THROUGH THE OPENING DOOR

My Pioneering Journey in Mainstream Journalism

NONA BALDWIN BROWN

iUniverse, Inc.
BLOOMINGTON

Through the Opening Door
My Pioneering Journey in Mainstream Journalism

iUniverse books may be ordered through booksellers or by contacting:

iUniverse
1663 Liberty Drive
Bloomington, IN 47403
www.iuniverse.com
1-800-Authors (1-800-288-4677)

ISBN: 978-1-4697-7184-7 (sc)
ISBN: 978-1-4697-7185-4 (ebk)

Library of Congress Control Number: 2012901940

Printed in the United States of America

iUniverse rev. date: 03/17/2012

IN GRATITUDE

This memoir is really a collaboration: Kerrie Baldwin, my great-niece, has done much to make it happen—from typing the manuscript to editorial direction and preparation for publication. Over three years of working with Kerrie, I've found her an excellent editor as well as a new friend.

Many, many thanks, Kerrie.

PREFACE

"Be careful. She's a very headstrong young lady!" Thus did my father warn my brand-new husband a few hours after we were married. Our wedding had taken place, with no advance planning, at the Church of the Transfiguration in midtown Manhattan the evening after Clinton and I decided, while dancing at the Stork Club, to get married and were persuaded to have a wedding right away, where we were both in uniform. This was not typical behavior for me! I thought of myself as orderly, quiet, and reliable. I had never been rebellious, unveiling only a mild ounce of independence when I dropped fourth-year Latin in favor of a typewriting class—and I thought that showed I was a practical, rational, clear-headed person.

Looking back at more than ninety years, I can see how this unique combination of personality traits served me well. Along with social and historical developments, and a bit of luck, I propelled my career in newspaper journalism, which spanned more than three decades. Although today my memory works fitfully, without much documented backup and likely in a self-serving manner, I can still recall my early childhood in the aftermath of World War I and then through nearly a century: I was a child in the Roaring Twenties, a teenager and college student through the Great Depression, an ensign in the navy in World War II, and a pioneer female reporter for *The New York Times* starting in 1940. I've witnessed the rise and fall of Marxist communism; the growth of women's rights, civil rights, and racial equality as political and social issues; and the invention of computers, leading to the globalization of economic forces. The path of my life has certainly been shaped and colored by the flow of the twentieth century, and it has always been busy—filled with friends and interesting people in American public life, a happy marriage, dozens of trips abroad (from India to the Amazon), and caring for my ailing father and Clinton's mother and aunt in our home. Here is my twentieth-century story.

CHAPTER 1

hildhood

From the beginning, my life was standard middle-class American. My parents, Helen Pugh Smitheman and Allen Thomas Baldwin, were both college graduates and from families with deep American roots. There were no famous ancestors—just a long roster of farmers, teachers, tradesmen, and lawyers active in local civic issues. Neither Mother nor Dad tended to talk much or tell colorful stories about their families. The Baldwin background became familiar to me mostly through frequent trips to West Chester, Pennsylvania, the center of the farming area where William Penn established a Quaker colony in the 1680s. My Baldwin ancestors worshiped, lived, and owned property during the last 300 years in several areas close to West Chester. Grandfather Thomas Webb Baldwin was the respected senior lawyer in the county court system when he died at ninety-six in 1948. His bedridden sister, Anne, still lived on the small family farm in nearby Romansville, which is now just a spot on the road, but I well remember the ramshackle house, barn, chicken yard, outhouse, open fields. That barnyard odor is still with me. My grandfather's other sister, Mary Prickett, eventually settled near West Chester, and so I came to know both her and her husband, Thomas. My grandfather's other siblings included (Joseph) Marion, a Philadelphia physician; (William) Herbert, a West Point graduate; and (Walter) John, who also had lived at the Romansville farm.

Occasionally, on these summer jaunts to West Chester, we would go to Philadelphia to see Mother's father and her married sister, Henrietta Clifton. Grandpa Smitheman, a widower, lived in a typical, small row house in west Philadelphia. There was not enough room to house us all, but I spent one memorable, sizzling hot night there, sleeping on a couch on the open front porch in order to get a breath of cool air. Aunt Henrietta was always a treat to visit; her townhouse was imaginatively decorated and comfortable, and she and her husband always had good nibbles to offer. They served alcoholic drinks, too, but not to my mother or to the children until I was in college. Uncle Bob Clifton was a bridge teacher; Aunt Hen was artistic and fun. She worked all her life as a secretary in the Philadelphia school system. They had one son, who lives with his large family in Wayne, Pennsylvania. He has worked diligently on the family genealogy.

On special expeditions we visited Anna Pierce, my mother's other sister. She lived in Haddonfield, New Jersey, with her husband and three daughters. My focus on these rare visits was really on becoming acquainted with my cousin, Margaret. A happy friendship evolved over the years, through her marriage and up to her premature death. (In the meantime, the slightly younger Pierce cousin, Anne, had married and moved with her husband, Lyman Wooster, to Fairfax, Virginia. Clinton and I were absorbed into their family of three children, especially at Thanksgiving and Christmas. Anne was a schoolteacher and Lyman a military researcher, both good conversationalists. (They now live in Hilton Head, South Carolina, and we check up on each other often by phone.)

Dad's mother, Lockey Ann Allen, came from a similar background: a pre-Revolutionary Quaker settlement near Burlington, New Jersey. She had graduated from a young ladies' finishing school and kept a rather literary notebook about her school years. I have only sketchy memories of her as a pleasant but firm mistress of her household. She died in 1927. A little later, my aunt Esther—a Swarthmore graduate—gave up her teaching job to stay home and help care for her father. During most of my childhood, this was the "family home" I knew. This semi-detached house on Walnut Street was large, with lots of bedrooms for a family of five.

Paternal grandparents Thomas Webb Baldwin and Lockey Ann Allen Baldwin in the garden of their 1885-1922 home at 207 West Gay Street, West Chester, PA

Clearly my paternal forebears were sober, industrious, steady people, dwelling generally within the purview of the West Chester Quarterly Meeting of the Society of Friends. By contrast, most of my maternal ancestors were city folk—namely Philadelphia, where my mother, Helen Pugh Smitheman, was born in 1890. Her father was a newcomer, born in Philadelphia to English parents who had been tavern keepers in Newcastle upon Tyne. Her mother, Henrietta Benonas Pugh, however, was a daughter of a leading Philadelphia family dating back to the Revolution. Her ancestor James Pugh was a manufacturer of heavy iron building equipment and supplier for Valley Forge.

Higher education didn't seem a strong Smitheman family interest—until my mother went to Bryn Mawr College, class of 1907. I was told that she was the first of her immediate family to attend college. I believe she earned some kind of scholarship from the Philadelphia public school system. Obviously, she was an exceptional student, excelling in Latin and mathematics, two fields she kept urging on me. I never heard her talk about dormitory life so I'm not sure whether she was a day student, traveling by streetcar to Bryn Mawr, or a boarding student, but she did make some lifelong friends from her undergraduate days.

My parents were married in Philadelphia in October 1911. We have no historical or photographic record of the event, but judging by the array of silver pieces featuring her maiden monogram, which were still with me until recently, the wedding must have been a big family affair. Their first home was in Cleveland, Ohio; Mother always spoke warmly of that life, especially because her first child was born there in 1913. I believe Dad was working for a cement factory as a metallurgist.

Parents Allen and Helen Baldwin, late 1920s

Nona as young toddler

I was born on May 11, 1918, in Elizabeth, New Jersey, an industrial/ railroad center with Atlantic Ocean port access and a small, pleasant residential area, where we lived. Dad commuted by train and ferry to New York City. I have no recollections of Elizabeth, but am told I had an Irish nursemaid, so my first baby words were in Irish brogue.

I'm not sure just why and when they moved to Elizabeth, though the cause was likely job related and due to our entry into World War I. When I arrived in May, my sister, Betty, was six years old. I have a few photographs showing me (in a carriage or someone's arms) and Betty and Mother, and the outdoor setting is pleasantly suburban.

The move to Montclair, just ten miles north, was prompted by the Pointville farm, which Dad had inherited some years earlier from his mother. Dad viewed the place as a financial drag and nuisance, so for years he tried

5

to sell it to his farm manager. Suddenly, on a Sunday afternoon in 1919, the farm manager appeared at our door in Elizabeth. He was ready to buy the farm—on the spot. Dad was pleased and willing to sign papers, but Mother (as she told the story) was cautious: *Why is he suddenly so eager to buy?* So they told the farm manager they wanted to think it over. The next day it was publicly announced that the federal government had condemned their land to add it to the huge Fort Dix army base. The government paid well!

This meant cash in hand for us, which led to the purchase of an attractive white clapboard house in Montclair and a handsome Nash touring car. Montclair was (and is today) a lovely bedroom community for New York City; it stretches along the eastern façade of the Watchung Mountains about fifteen miles west of Manhattan. The population then was about 25,000.

Our house was a roomy, three-story frame building with five bedrooms, two baths, and a full basement with coal furnace, coal bin, and a gas hot-water heater that had to be lit with a match. We had a garage, an apple tree outside the dining room, and plenty of space for flower beds and croquet games. This was my world from kindergarten through high school—my whole childhood and adolescence.

During the next two decades, the Baldwin family loomed larger in my life than the Smithemans. The large West Chester house was about four hours' drive from Montclair, and, after Lockey Ann's death, that household consisted of Grandfather, still active as a lawyer, and Aunt Esther. (I never knew Dad's other sibling, John, who postponed his law studies to go into the army. He was killed in battle just weeks before the Armistice on November 11, 1918.)

Esther was a teacher in Philadelphia and at the West Chester Normal School (now West Chester University). She taught me to be a proper Quaker: to use "thee" and "thou" in family conversation; to learn about George Fox, the founder; to sit quietly through Sunday morning services; and to look at the world with friendly eyes. She also loved to tickle me and then giggle at my laughter. She had been relatively independent in her youth, even going to London with the Red Cross after the war. Reading to children was a favorite activity for her—and the children lucky enough to hear her. She never married, and around 1935 she gave up her teaching career to care for her father, who was slowly becoming deaf and blind. He died, at 96, in 1948.

Home life through these years was comfortable and relaxed. Mother and Father were always even tempered, warm hearted, and sometimes even stimulating, but rarely was the house full of laughter or loving warmth. They were quite Victorian in their attitudes; they never argued in front of us, and neither ever told me about the birds and the bees. I had to deal with all those strange elements of adolescence by myself. (When I was sixteen, Mother did once tell me never to let a boy touch me. She never told me why.)

We always took a summer vacation, even through the Depression, spending two to three weeks in places ranging from Maine, Martha's Vineyard, Peconic Bay on Long Island, and especially to Lavalette and other resorts on the New Jersey shore. I attended a Girl Scout camp for two summers, learning such skills as life-saving swimming, making my own bow and arrow, and dealing with bullying.

The world was becoming larger—and closer. The new reign of the automobile infused so many aspects of family life with mobility and change, making an easy adventure for a middle-class family with three children to travel relatively enormous distances for summer vacations. Our new car was a glorious machine, with front and back seats and a contraption for installing Isinglass and screen windows. Making that seasonal change in the Nash windows could guarantee harsh purple language from my normally mild-spoken father.

The Depression years were sobering. I knew something had happened to Dad, who no longer brought home the fanciest new radio and no longer worked for General Electric. He tried to do consulting work, which finally led to a job with the Hanson-Van Winkle-Munning Company, a chemical manufacturer. Pay was low and sporadic, even through the late '30s. We all learned to "make do" and bought very few new clothes. I darned any holes in my stockings, including long runs up the legs. I learned to save a little every week from my school lunch allowance and put those pennies in the bank. This habit of saving even small amounts is still part of my routine; I pay cash or personal check for everything from a new car to my rent. Installment buying was never for me.

Later, Dad had to borrow those bank savings to pay an emergency medical bill for Mother, who had developed severe influenza and rheumatoid arthritis. This was the start of Mother's invalidism, which lasted the rest of her life. Dad took wonderful, loving care of Mother through many downs and ups until her death in 1958. In the final years, he had enough money to indulge her, even taking her to England to visit friends and buying her a full-length black sealskin coat one winter.

The most sobering development was the need to bring Grandfather Smitheman to live with us in 1932. He had been a food broker—with no buyers. Since Mother could offer him our spare bedroom, we were all pleased to have him join the family. He was a jolly, pipe-smoking guy, not very tall but very friendly. He never understood—and often joked about—Mother's strong aversion to alcoholic drinks. At Christmastime he quickly accepted a neighbor's invitation to share some eggnog and other libations, teasing her as he went out the door. Later, when he fell ill, our doctor prescribed a stimulant before his dinner every night; Dad immediately drove to a newly opened liquor store (this was 1933) and came home with a bottle of sherry. Mother frowned. Grandpa grinned. He would go to the pantry cupboard each evening, pour himself his drink, and then walk around the house to find Mother and offer her a sip. He was with us until his death from cancer in 1935.

There wasn't much entertaining in our house, and Betty and Tom and I—each six years apart—did not have friends in common. As a family, we did play checkers, Parcheesi, Ouija, and auction bridge with Mother and Dad. (I had learned to play bridge at eight years old during a vacation rainy spell at Peconic Bay.) We all had household roles: Mother cooked dinner, and Betty and I shared the clean-up chores. Housecleaning, laundry, weeding, sewing, and mending were handled mostly by the distaff crew, though Dad—with help from Tom—usually mowed the grass, did heavy yard work, and dealt with the coal furnace and plumbing. We had no hired help during the '30s.

Somehow I became the fancy cook in our family. I loved cooking then and still would if I could. By my high school years, I regularly spent Saturday morning making nut bread or a layer cake, maybe devil's food with white frosting for our Sunday dinner. But it was Mother who created our one outstanding culinary treasure: she tried to make ice cream as directed for our brand-new electric refrigerator. What we were served was unidentifiable slush and quickly christened "alibi ice" by Dad. It remained a family joke for years. Normally, our menus were good old-fashioned beef and lamb, potatoes, scrapple and waffles, rice pudding and baked custard. And always Waldorf salad (made by Dad!) for Sunday evening supper.

Nona as teenager

Two teachers, one in junior high and one in senior, sparked my lifelong interest in music, mostly as a listener. In ninth grade, the music teacher chose me (of all people) to sing a solo at the Christmas special assembly that year. With shaky bravado, I did it. Mother and Betty were in the audience, nervous and tense, and they finally let themselves breathe again after I finished. This was considered an extraordinary and unexpected "first" for anyone in the Baldwin family. I went on to a little voice training as well as glee club singing in high school; later, in college, I also studied music history. My contralto voice has morphed into its current cackle.

Another high school teacher made a more enduring impact on my life's path. After reading through one of my homework assignments, she remarked, "You would make a good reporter. That's what you should do."

9

Although I had done some paste-up work on *The Mountaineer*, our high school newspaper, I didn't know what reporting truly entailed, but that sentence stuck in my head and steered me toward my lifelong career in journalism. Since I wasn't an athlete or an actress, the newspaper was just about the only extracurricular activity left for me during high school. I was automatically subordinated to the boys who were the top editors, but that never bothered me. As through my adult career, I simply worked hard in my position on the student paper, and from the local paper *The Montclair Times* I received a medallion for excellence in journalism.

I don't recall anything about attending my senior prom, but I must have: there is a photograph of me in what was surely my prom gown. Boys didn't play much of a role in my life at that time. I was friendly with many classmates—boys and girls, white and black, Italian and Jewish—without becoming socially popular, maybe because I was taller than most boys my age, or because I had no athletic prowess and was a rather big, hefty teenager, or because there was no girl close to my age in my neighborhood. However, I was, I thought, perfectly happy. And I must have had plenty of self-confidence, since I sailed through the Montclair public school system, which has always ranked among the best in the country. My string of A-filled report cards was briefly interrupted in high school, when an English teacher scolded me for laziness and gave me a B.

In those high school years, I may have demonstrated that "headstrong" trait in my decisions to drop fourth-year Latin and to apply to Vassar College instead of Bryn Mawr. Mother and Dad were not pleased by these deviations, but they did not attempt to stop me or argue me out of my preferences. The Depression had taught us practicality, and Vassar had lower housing costs than Bryn Mawr. Betty had never made her college education—or campus life—seem the least bit stimulating. She had an active social life thanks to her friend Kathleen (Kay) Pickell, who was a lively party girl with strong connections to the boys at Theta Xi at Lehigh College. Kay arranged a couple of blind-date weekends for Betty, where she met and fell in love with Frank Montbach. So when Betty graduated in 1934, already pinned and engaged to marry, she took a quick typing course and got a clerical job to fill the time before their wedding in August 1936. I did not have a boyfriend and did not consider marriage my postgraduate goal. Journalism seemed a more interesting way to earn a living than a secretarial job.

In my mind, Vassar College offered a much more exciting prospect: a mix of students from all over New England and New York and an atmosphere more sophisticated and somehow more glamorous. The only girl I knew—and I didn't know her well—who had attended Vassar was the daughter of family friends who happened to be richer and more socially connected than others. Best of all, Vassar's dormitory rooms were distributed by lottery rather than by price (Betty lived in the cheapest dorm closet for her four years at Bryn Mawr and I suspect this influenced her general outlook).

So, in 1935, off to Vassar I went. At the time, college admission was less complicated than today. I applied only to Vassar, passed the standard admission test, and was duly accepted. College then cost $1200 a year for room, board, and tuition. Even that was hard to come by, so I was granted a small but crucial stipend from an education fund of the Montclair Friends Meeting.

CHAPTER 2

$\mathscr{B}$rain Training

Suddenly I was in a new world. And I was by myself.

The Vassar campus, well separated from the shabby city of Poughkeepsie, was like a verdant village: acres of trees and green lawns dotted by its gothic library, classic steepled church, landmark main administration building, and scattered dormitory and academic buildings all connected by foot and bicycle paths. My dormitory, Davison, was a dull old structure in a quadrangle of matching dormitories. But the people inside that unimpressive building—perhaps 50 students, including juniors and sophomores as well as incoming freshmen—were a lively, friendly mixture of attractive young women. To me, the atmosphere was all so new, so sophisticated; yet I felt at ease quickly and the older students helped me get settled.

By luck, my room was a single. Vassar's dorm assignments were made by lottery, so there was no distinction between "rich" and "poor" girls. In my mind, this was one of the best aspects of Vassar's educational planning. I had always studied alone, and I wasn't sure how to mix with new girls, but I made several friends quite quickly, and three of these early friendships—Charlotte Remington, Caroline Stearns, and Ruth Frankenthaler—lasted until their deaths in recent years.

It was Ruth who asked me shyly if I would accompany her to synagogue for Rosh Hashanah services that evening. "Of course," I said, and off we went by taxi. We drew up to the rather grimy building in downtown Poughkeepsie, and Ruth seemed unnerved by the scruffy appearance of the synagogue. When we entered and were ushered to a balcony overlooking the main floor, Ruth was puzzled and distressed. The floor was a dreary chamber holding many groups, male and female, walking around and apparently chatting. I had never before been inside a synagogue and had no idea what to expect. But Ruth did know what *she* expected, and this wasn't it. So we returned immediately to college, and Ruth, upset, phoned her mother. The next week her mother drove to Vassar to take Ruth back to New York City for Yom Kippur. This was a learning experience for me. I felt totally comfortable as I faced, for the first time, a stranger with a different religion and a very sophisticated personality.

I came to Vassar with no major field of study in mind, but I soon settled on English with a special interest in journalism. Later I added economics as my minor. My freshman and sophomore studies were drawn from the traditional liberal curriculum: English, history, economics, psychology, French, German, and physical education. I managed to persuade the authorities that, despite that A in high school physics, I had no aptitude or interest in the hard sciences or advanced math.

Academically, I stumbled badly during both freshman and sophomore years. My grades were uniformly Cs for all subjects until the second half of sophomore year, when two cheerful Bs appeared on my report card. I was finally learning not only how to study but also to find excitement in the pleasure of learning. And I knew I was competing with a lot of students far brighter and better prepared than I.

I also began to recognize the Depression's effect on everyday life, including my family's. I learned not only to be thrifty, but, more importantly, that I would probably have to work for a living after I graduated. My parents often questioned my curious interest in becoming a journalist but never doubted my assumed need to enter the workforce. In this, I was probably ahead of the economic curve, as I wondered how my Vassar courses would prepare me to earn a living after graduation. Many of us discussed this topic rather often, but apparently my personal worries reached the college dean, C. Mildred Thompson. One day I was summoned to her office and told, rather sternly, that if getting a job was my educational goal then I was in the wrong place. "This is the place to learn to think," she lectured. She invited me to go elsewhere! I was stunned. And embarrassed. I had no intention of leaving Vassar—and I was just beginning to get excited about new knowledge.

As a top-ranked liberal college for women, with a faculty attuned to the violent economic and political changes occurring around the globe,

Vassar was the right place for me at the moment. My vocabulary—as well as my studying—began to include the great intellectual developments and minds and economic theories of modern western European history: the Renaissance, the Enlightenment, democracy, Christianity, Marxism, Adam Smith, John Maynard Keynes, and fascism. For me, the world opened up, both intellectually and geographically.

In the summer of 1937, I had the eye-opening experience of spending six weeks in Flint, Michigan. There, in the huge Buick factory—now silent—the great workers' sit-down strike had helped to ignite industrial labor unions and their right to organize for labor's rights. As an American Friends Service Committee student, I worked with some of the damaged people and other detritus of the Depression, including mass unemployment in the auto industry, the indifference of larger corporations to the needs of their employees, and the strikes and battles of the new CIO. That summer kick-started my lifelong concern about economic fairness for the working-class citizens of our country.

This and other human rights issues encouraged much of the campus, faculty and students alike, to speak out about the Spanish Civil War (anti-Franco sentiment was strong, although the "red" Soviet Union was also supporting the anti-Franco forces) and the great street battles and political uproar over FDR and the New Deal program. I was one of many Vassar students who slipped away from family Republicanism into a more liberal political philosophy. When FDR came to Poughkeepsie in 1936 on the day after his reelection, a huge student crowd went downtown to see and cheer him with the kind of excited enthusiasm seen in the first Obama campaign. Seemingly the whole campus was excited about the New Deal and the direction of the country still sobered by Depression.

But we had our fun, anyway, whether going to an experimental theater show, to the movie off campus, for a quick bite at an off-campus coffee shop, to enjoy a short round of golf, or just for long walks around our campus's hundreds of acres. I ventured off campus socially only four times in four years: once to Dartmouth, once to Colgate, and twice to Williams. I indeed had a boyfriend at Williams and he came to Vassar for senior prom. (We lost touch soon after, but I know he shortly joined the Marine Corps.)

My membership on the board of Vassar's *Miscellany News* was, of course, my main non-academic job. The *Misc*, like many college papers, was a weekly publication and its editors had strong opinions on ways to correct the ills of the world. Several of my colleagues were true radicals—very bright, articulate activists. Most of the *Misc* consisted of routine bulletin announcements and reports of ordinary events, but the top editors (of which I was not one) usually handled the editorial of the week, sometimes opining about the hot-button radical issue of the moment. When work was finished, we would all sit around the big table in an office in Students' Building, quaff a beer, and then offer a loud rendition of the proletarian marching song, "Workers of the World, Unite!" Since I am by instinct a non-joiner—I don't like to wear any labels for or against a cause—I just listened and learned. This was another part of the real world—all so very new to me.

I had one brief interruption in my junior year: I was hit by a car! A friend on the *Misc* board invited me and another colleague to visit her over a weekend at her home in a village east of Albany. Her father drove down to Vassar to pick us up. After a wonderful home-cooked meal with her family, we three Vassar girls went for a stroll "downtown"—we walked three abreast in the gravelly shoulders of the quiet, two-lane country road, heading for the general store. Suddenly, I was facedown in the gravel. An old man, nearly blind, had sneaked his family Model T out of the barn to go for a jaunt. The car hit me on the back of my legs when, he claimed, he swerved to avoid a dog. I was not seriously hurt; the damage was severe leg bruising—and the loss of a front tooth! To this day—seventy years later—I wear a special gold bridge in my mouth to hold a replacement tooth. Dad did his best to get the family of the driver, who had no license, to help pay for my dental repair. I believe we finally got $200.

Senior year was largely consumed by writing my thesis or term paper for my senior seminar class, "The Contemporary Press." My professor was Helen D. Lockwood, a brilliant, outspoken, stimulating teacher. We personally didn't get along so famously, mostly because she did not like journalistic writing, but her counsel—to "avoid stereotyping" people and ideas—has been a guiding light for me ever since. Somehow I produced seventy typewritten pages, complete with footnotes and bibliography, titled "Edmund Wilson: 20th Century Critic." As I reread it today, I wonder how I ever had the time, patience, vocabulary, and typing accuracy to produce such an impressive document.

By this time, I had come to recognize the truth of Dean Thompson's admonition. Now I knew how very much I didn't know—about fine arts, drama, music, philosophy, and science. But my experience at Vassar fortified my interest in journalism, not so much as a vocation but as a way to know the world better. And I realized that, through graduate school, I could gain the professional tools that Dean Thompson so caustically consigned to vocational schools. I was accepted by, and registered for, the Columbia University Graduate School of Journalism to start in September 1939.

Part of this new life ahead, I decided, must include the traditional college graduation gift of a trip around Europe. Mother and Dad supported this fantasy mostly by helping with the practical side: arranging tickets, itinerary, and such. To fund the adventure I used part of my remaining educational trust money plus the leftover spending money I had earned at college. Virginia Snead, a friend and neighbor from Montclair, helped with arranging details, and my classmate Caroline Stearns planned to join us in Innsbruck, Austria, after completing a swing through Russia with her grandfather.

Our itinerary was a whopper: six weeks, six countries, all carefully scheduled and reserved: England, Belgium, Germany (Rhine River, Heidelberg, Munich), Austria, Italy (Venice, Lake Como, Milan), Switzerland (Geneva), and France (Paris). (My recollection is that the total cost was about $800.) The *Queen Mary* would carry us to England; the brand-new *Mauritania* would provide the return trip in September. There was a very noisy rumble about possible war, but we were told that as long as the "talks" involving Germany and Poland continued with England and France as guarantors of Poland's safety, nothing bad would happen.

On July 10, Ginny and I and the *Queen Mary* sailed away. Our six-week adventure began quietly, routinely. We headed to England first, where we hit all the tourist high spots of London—the crown jewels at the Tower, St. Paul's Cathedral, Westminster Abbey, and Buckingham Palace—plus Stonehenge and Stratford. Then Ginny and I crossed the English Channel at Margate and headed via Belgium to Cologne, where we boarded a Rhine River steamer. This took us to the fascinating old University of Heidelberg, then on to Munich by train. Ginny, who knew more about operas and museums than I, got us tickets for a performance of *Der Meistersinger*. My first exposure to grand opera was a stunning experience.

In Munich we finally found crowds of other tourists—mostly American students—who collected each night at the famous Hofbräuhaus, a many-roomed, multi-storied palace for beer by the liter, wursts and cheeses of all kinds, quick service, and high-decibel oompa music. It was exciting.

One evening I remembered a special request from my brother-in-law, Mal, whose parents were German: "Please, would you bring me a stein from the Hofbräuhaus?" No sooner remembered than done. I sequestered *three* steins, one glass and two ceramic, with the famous logo. I am embarrassed to admit that I held all three of the one-liter jugs under my tweed coat and waddled out of the place, pretending to be very pregnant. No questions were asked and all three of the steins eventually arrived in Montclair. The unusual glass stein, a prized possession, remained with me until five years ago when I passed it along to a nephew who likes beer as much as his father did.

Also in Munich I experienced my first real taste of Nazism. A German exchange student, whom I had known in Montclair and kept in touch with over the years, asked me to join him for lunch one day. As we walked through central Munich, we approached the Feldherrnhalle, the imposing building where Hitler had made his historic oration to launch his Nazi march to power. The building had become a Nazi national shrine. My friend, Eugen, saluted and called on me to do the same. I refused—and that was the last I saw of him. I have often wondered whether Eugen survived the war and if he ever realized what Nazism meant.

Innsbruck, Austria, was next on our itinerary. Here, Ginny and I were joined by my college classmate Caroline ("Care") Stearns. We lingered a day or two and then the three of us took the train to Venice, via Milan. The fourth seat in our compartment was occupied by a handsome young German student, self-assured with his English and proud of his architectural scholarship to study in Rome. He took a shine to me, so he followed us to Venice from Milan and booked himself into our hotel, to the dismay of the three of us. By now, his Nazi ideas were proudly on display and I didn't quite know how to deal with his arrogance. On that first evening in Venice, Ginny, Care, and I were quietly enjoying a few minutes on the hotel veranda facing the Grand Canal when the young architect appeared, and he proceeded to extol the Nazi weltanschauung. Luckily for me, also on the porch was an older American tour guide—a classicist and Harvard graduate who rose to the challenge. A loud debate ensued. The ill-informed German student finally left the scene, unable to face robust criticism for the first time and muttering about American rudeness and stupidity. Ginny, Care, and I were silently grateful and enjoyed the rest of the evening. The next morning, the German found me in the dining room and asked why I had not stopped that awful man who had been so rude to him. I replied, in effect, that he needed to hear criticism of his view of the world and to learn that much of the world considered Hitler and Nazism politically and socially wrong. I suppose he left Venice on the next train.

The possibility of war kept growing, but we had no solid source of information. So on we went, to Milan and then to Lake Como, where we stayed at the famous Villa Serbelloni. It was a glorious spot with a luxurious, almost empty hotel. This was mid-August, normally a peak month for tourism. There were few guests in the dining room, but a formal panoply of waiters attended us, anyway. Next, we traveled by boat through the Italian lakes to Stresa and then by train to Geneva. This time the train was jam-packed with English citizens who had all been ordered home by the British government. The three of us stayed in Geneva for a couple of days and finally reached Paris around August 26.

Needless to say, the mood on the train was somber. "They" were still talking, we were told, but no one knew who was saying what or what might be the result. So when we got settled in our small hotel near the Café de la Paix, I went to the Chase National Bank to present my letter of introduction to a friend of one of my Montclair neighbors. Lucky for us, my parents had insisted on this letter, just in case we had any trouble. The man at Chase turned us over to the care of an Anglo-French lawyer named François Monahan, whose American secretary had family living just outside Paris.

On September 1, the Germans invaded Poland; France and England declared war on Germany; and everyone's life changed abruptly. Actually, nothing happened in Paris, but apparently French officialdom felt positive that Paris would be hit by German bombers immediately, so every time a German plane crossed the Maginot Line, all the air-raid sirens screamed and the populace scrambled into air-raid shelters, often in the basements of office buildings.

We went into one such "*abri*" under the Chase Bank. François and his secretary urged us to leave the city immediately and go to Malesherbes, where a Mme. Blanc was caring for the secretary's children and would provide safe shelter for us. We took that advice. We stayed at the boys' school (in chicken houses transformed into schoolrooms) for four or five days, until François phoned to tell us to return to Paris. The city was safe he said, and we could travel to England from there.

But we couldn't. A night in Paris, a crowded trip on the boat train to the port of Le Havre, and then a great big NO sign greeted us: our peacetime visas were no good. Because of the state of war, we couldn't get to England and our tickets on the *Mauritania* were useless. At about 6 p.m. we turned to the U.S. consulate for help. We waited anxiously for the consul, but he was totally occupied by a phone conversation another man was having with a senator in Washington. The man on the phone was repeating to the senator that there was no way he could provide a stateroom for two important ladies. When this phone call ended, the man turned to us and asked pleasantly, "And what can I do for you, young ladies?" Alas, I have forgotten the name of this Samaritan, who was head of the United States Lines office in Le Havre. He explained that two ships would be coming into port over the weekend. Yes, he could take care of us, as long as we didn't mind sleeping on cots in the mail room of one of these ships. He would exchange our Cunard Line tickets for U.S. Line tickets at no charge. "Glad to help you," he said. "Just come by my office in the morning and I'll take care of you."

The next morning, it was easy to locate the U.S. Line office: a big building on a public plaza packed tight with perhaps 5,000 Americans—from all over Europe—pushing and talking. The main office door was tightly guarded. We were standing in line when suddenly Care, who was six feet tall, scanned the crowd and ducked out. A few minutes later, a piece of white note paper was passed down to me: *The ack-bay oor-day is down the street on your left.—Care.* Ginny and I understood the pig latin, found the basement entrance, and showed up on the main floor to be greeted by Care and our new friend, the boss. In no time he had changed our tickets to depart on the SS *Washington* on September 12. We were indeed quartered in the mail room, well below normal passenger levels. With new tickets in hand, we searched and found better (not bed-bugged) overnight accommodations and enjoyed what amounted to a refugee block party for a couple of days.

Nona (second from left), Bobby Kennedy (in necktie, behind net), and Kathleen Kennedy (in head scarf) playing handball on top deck of SS Washington, 1939

The SS *Washington* was a modest ocean liner with a capacity of 1100 passengers. By the time it absorbed all the refugees from France and England, about 2200 people were onboard. These included Mrs. Rose Kennedy and three of her children; Donald Budge and Bill Tilden, the reigning world tennis champions; the violinist Fritz Kreisler; and the author Thomas Mann. From our basement cots we could climb the back stairways into the second- or first-class precincts—and this we did all the time. I played pick-up bridge with some international lawyers in first class and played handball with Bobby Kennedy and his sister on the top deck, on which a large American flag had been painted to announce our neutrality. We just mingled with the crowds and enjoyed ourselves. Personally, I made one true friendship then, with a Harvard graduate student named James Tobin. Later, when we both ended up in Washington in 1942, Jim and I dated frequently. He went on to fame as an economist and won the Nobel Prize in Economics in 1981.

As I remember those tumultuous weeks—from Germany to Le Havre—I do not recall any sense of panic or worry among the three of us. The whole summer had been truly so much fun, we had met so many friendly people, and we at no point felt threatened. The start of hostilities seemed to make no difference at the Café de la Paix, where boy met girl and small talk grew in minutes into friendship. A Harvard graduate and I fell into a quick rapport, but he had passage back to the United States on August 31. We exchanged addresses, and when I finally arrived in New York on September 17 my mother was on the pier, demanding to know who this Harvard boy was! He had sent me a chatty letter that sent my mother's Victorian imagination flying. I did see this friend later in the fall, but the romantic summer moment had passed.

Seemingly the next day I started classes at Columbia's Graduate School of Journalism. By some miracle I already had a place to live at the university: Jean Davidson, a Vassar classmate, was attending Columbia Law and had rented an apartment for the two of us just a block from campus. So that very comfortable, convenient abode became home for the next ten months.

There were sixty-five students in my class at the journalism school, about fifteen of them women. It was a diverse group: some older, experienced reporters seeking training along with raw beginners like me. We were a friendly bunch. In addition to learning to become professional journalists, we partied together, such as the tense night when five or six of us decided to explore 125th Street in Harlem, just down the hill through Morningside Park. This area was considered high-risk territory.

Our instructors were working journalists, like the city editor of *The New York Times*, and they worked us hard. The curriculum included studying the role and goal for good journalism as well as reporting assignments around the city. We learned from prominent writers, such as Douglas Southall Freeman, Walter Pitkin, and Henry Pringle, about the historic importance of good journalism in our democratic society; to be as objective as possible in all writing; to check and recheck all facts; and to be alert to the world around us as well as the whole panorama of our own country.

This led to plenty of serious thinking (and arguing) about hot topics, such as the 1940 election debates, civil rights' issues, and war threats. "Women's page" or society journalism was never mentioned. One day I was assigned to cover the Earl Browder trial and another assignment sent me to a slum area for a piece on a new educational program. We were also exposed to what was then the "new media": television and radio reporting.

At the end of this intense year, we all were required to produce a thesis on some aspect of the news. I chose labor reporting because of my experience in Flint and the dominance of labor problems as major public issues. But that opus was never written.

In early April, *New York Times* Sunday Editor Lester Markel requested four students to help for a couple of weeks with the detail work of updating the *Times'* guide to the 1939 World's Fair for 1940. Carl Ackerman, dean of the J-school, asked for volunteers, and I got one of the jobs! It was dull, fact-checking work, but it was exciting to be on 43rd Street and working for the *Times!* After two weeks, Mr. Markel asked two of us to stay two weeks longer, so it was early May before I finally returned to 116th Street. The atmosphere at school had changed; most of my classmates had already completed their theses and were job hunting.

Finding a job seemed to me my most pressing problem. Remembering one professor's job-hunting advice—to approach any editor and offer whatever special expertise you had—I marched myself back down to the *Times* and asked Mr. Markel if he thought I could get a job on the *NYT* World's Fair staff that summer. Markel replied, "Why not?" and made a date for me to see the managing editor. If memory serves correctly, I met him (Jimmy James) and his assistant, Bruce Rae, that same day. And almost the next day I was hired! I was also asked to be ready to start work the following week. Stunned and elated, I raced back to school to find high-pitch excitement in the air over the forthcoming Pulitzer Prizes—not the famous ones for press excellence but the three travel fellowships awarded each year to J-school graduates with financing for nine months of foreign travel. This unusual fellowship stemmed from Joseph Pulitzer's firm belief that Americans should have much better information about the rest of the world and that good journalism from experienced reporters would provide this. I returned uptown in high excitement over my spectacular new job when I learned that I was one of the recipients of a Pulitzer fellowship. I was surprised, giddy with disbelief, and hardly knew which way to turn. I think Jean took me out for a drink and dinner that night, and I phoned Mother and Dad. My parents had moved to Red Bank, New Jersey, because of Mother's health, and they were too far away (and Mother too unwell) to come into the city for any grand celebration.

I knew that the two awards required quick decisions, so I turned to Dean Ackerman. First we talked about the *New York Times* job and the paper's request that I start work the next week. Dean Ackerman was so pleased by the job—he said it was the first such direct hire from the J-school by the *Times* in many years—that he just waved me on, saying not to worry about the thesis and go ahead and start work on May 20. And he added that, of course, I would get my master's degree. He told me I did not need to write a thesis or finish classes; my employment by the *Times* was evidence enough that I had learned what the school was designed to teach. Thank you, Dean Ackerman. Then I asked about the fellowship's proviso that it must be used in the next academic year, which would begin before the end of 1940. The dean advised me simply to wait; no decision was needed until September or October. That year, the *Times* included the three Pulitzer travel fellowship winners in their full report on the major prizes—with pictures! I was overwhelmed by all the attention.

I began working on May 20 on the *NYT* World's Fair staff. This was Opening Day, and I was assigned to cover the crowds at the main gate. I honestly don't remember details of the scene, but when I arrived at a typewriter in the temporary *NYT* bureau, I wrote a simple 300-word what-when-where-who-why story about the overflow crowd. The editor seemed pleased and added it to incoming copy from other areas of the fair. He ended up using my lede for the big story of the day and told me later he thought it could have been written by a man. That was meant as a compliment.

I had been at the job for only two weeks when I was transferred to the main city staff on 43rd Street—a huge room, almost as large as a city block, filled with men, desks, buzzing phones, typewriters, and strangers. The desk to which I was assigned was next to Kathleen McLaughlin, an experienced reporter (and good friend, later) hired recently from the *Chicago Tribune*. Along the 43rd Street side of the room, the offices of the managing editor, assistant managing editor, and city editor were ranged; the copy desk was in front of the desk of the city editor, David H. Joseph, to whom I would report for assignments. Three of us—Kathleen, the secretary to Managing Editor Jimmy James, and I, a cub reporter—were the only women in the room! This somehow didn't faze me. Some of the male reporters were friendly and welcoming; some obviously were unhappy with my presence. My own behavior was carefully ladylike but casual: neatly dressed, friendly, and professional. As a result, I soon developed working relationships with my colleagues, dated two or three of these men socially, and finally was even asked to join one of the male lunchtime groups. This, as far as I was concerned, was professional acceptance.

During the next months, I had several special assignments among the daily trivia: I went to Vassar College to cover the commencement speaker (President Mildred McAfee of Wellesley), only one year after my own graduation, which generated lots of raised eyebrows and much amusement from my friends on the college staff as well as several professors. The news report in the paper was short, as usual. On the rare occasion when Mrs. Wendell Willkie was in the city, I covered her activities. She was a charming lady, generally uninterested in politics, and had little to say about her husband's campaign against FDR. I have a photo of one of these occasional press conferences—which drew maybe a half dozen reporters. Mrs. Willkie and I were the only women in the group—par for the course in 1940.

*Nona (center) and male newspaper and wire service reporters interviewing
Mrs. Wendell Willkie, 1940*

Mrs. Willkie was no newsmaker, but indirectly she gave me a major boost on Election Day. I had reported her routine behind-the-scenes all day and her final stop at Willkie headquarters in the Hotel Commodore. I was in the ballroom, with all the national press, awaiting Wendell Willkie's inevitable concession speech. Willkie didn't concede anything that night, so he and his wife didn't make a press appearance. I headed back across town to the *Times* and went straight to the city room, where the first (10 p.m.) edition was available, and there was my story—with my byline! I really couldn't believe my eyes. I must have shrieked in my excitement. A colleague cooled me down quickly: I was standing next to the publisher, Arthur Hays Sulzberger, who was deep in a critical assessment of the overall political coverage. He probably never even noticed me, thank goodness. In those days, bylines on news stories, especially local ones, were very rare, and certainly never expected on any routine metro story. I don't know what prompted it, but that news clip is one of my treasures, my proof that I really worked for *The New York Times* in 1940.

Right after that startling event, I resigned from the *Times*. With Bruce Rae's urging, I had decided to accept the Pulitzer fellowship and I prepared to embark for a nine-month trip to South America on November 15.

Latin America would not have been my first choice for nearly a year of traveling, listening, and learning, but World War II had ruled out Europe. South America was unknown territory to me and most Americans, but the locale turned out to be perfect: it opened up a very different world, where I met hundreds of new people, heard new (to me) languages, witnessed rich and colorful unexpected beauty and unbelievable squalor, and gained a superficial view of the political and economic differences among the four countries I visited. There was no tourism, no clusters of vacationing Americans, and, in some areas, more sympathy for the German than the British and French cause during the war.

Brazil was first and most important on my itinerary, and it was scheduled for at least three months' visit. Buenos Aires, Argentina; Santiago, Chile; and Lima, Peru were allotted about three weeks each. Grace Line ocean liners provided most transportation, including seventeen days each way at sea. My friend Jean Davidson took a year off from law school and volunteered to accompany me for the entire journey. After the ships rolled in a stormy sea off the East Coast for a few days, we emerged from our stateroom to greet fellow passengers and size them up. And so the fun and education began. There were, of course, many Brazilian, Argentine, and Chilean business travelers, but also quite a number of sophisticated Europeans who presumably had business interests in Rio or Buenos Aires.

There were just a few Americans, either businessmen or government workers, and no sightseers.

The *Santa Maria* offered all the amenities of a cruise ship: swimming pool, games, dancing, bars, and legions of deck chairs. English was the common language, so we quickly became acquainted with everyone. With day after day of tropical sunshine, the swimming pool became the social center. Jean and I each got ceremoniously dunked as we crossed the equator, and of course we often joined other activities. On the night of the traditional costume party, Jean worked up a sports outfit and I put on a Bavarian dirndl that I had bought in 1939 in Innsbruck. We were all having fun until an Austrian named Fritz Mandel accosted me with voluble German and French. His interest, inflamed by my innocent *mädchen* appearance, was clear: he wished for me to come with him to his stateroom. As I started moving away from his heavy-handed approaches, he began chasing me—and almost caught me just as I reached my stateroom door and entered it safely alone. I later learned that Heddy Lamar, the Madonna of her day, was his wife. Whew! Another shipboard friend was a very dignified and courteous elderly gentleman named Walter Lubovich. He liked our company, so he always—and frequently—entertained Jean and me together. (To see me alone, he explained to me, would lead to endless shipboard gossip that he wished to avoid.) He also gave me a clear look at the social mores of international society: his daughter, he said, was a huge disappointment to him, since after marrying very well to an exemplary Italian count she had refused to take a lover. He felt she would lose social stature if she did not—and this wounded his pride.

In Argentina, Chile, and Peru, I caught only a quick glimpse of each capital city, and with the striking exception of Peru, that was my focus. But Brazil was special for me—I would have time to see and learn much, and hopefully do some reporting. There Frank Garcia, *New York Times* resident correspondent, was expecting me, and he and his wife made me feel more comfortable in a strange setting. They even provided Christmas dinner for us. But he couldn't do anything about the beastly December heat!

In Rio, we started out in a small hotel on Copacabana beach but soon moved to a lovely apartment near Sugarloaf that belonged to a *LIFE* photographer and his wife. I soon connected with a number of resident Americans, notably Harry Bagley, the Associated Press bureau chief; and Bennett Cave, an engineer with GE, with whom I became good friends.

In other capitals, I was not so lucky in meeting and socializing with contemporary young professionals, but in Chile I was truly befriended by one Chilean family, and in Peru a lovely American Embassy wife took me to a charity school for slum children and then arranged a trip into the Andes for us.

With Frank Garcia's guidance, I registered at the press office of the foreign ministry and then made my first reportorial request: to interview Sra. Darci Vargas, wife of the president (and dictator) of Brazil, General Getúlio Vargas, to report on her charity work in the *favellas* of the country. These slums surrounding the city were shantytowns overflowing the valleys and hills, bursting with the impoverished and illiterate millions. These *favellas* were also full of native music and gave birth to the samba—creating samba schools and the imaginatively colorful floats featured in the Carnival parade every year.

My interview request seemed to get lost in the bureaucracy, but eventually Frank phoned me to say the meeting was all set for one day in January. Accompanied by Frank, I took the train to Petrópolis, the nearby mountain resort that serves as the summer capital. Upon arrival at the mansion, we were ushered into a lounge, and then, finally, the door to an office opened and we were escorted in—to meet President Vargas! There was no sign or mention of Sra. Vargas. The general and I exchanged pleasantries, with Frank explaining who I was and why I was in Brazil. I was identified as Doctora Baldwin, in deference to my unusual (for a woman) professional status. After perhaps five minutes, we left and took the train back to Rio. The next day, the major newspapers of Rio printed the photo of General Vargas and Doctora Baldwin on the front page. The Vargas publicity machine was at work: it was the mandatory Vargas picture of the day.

Eventually, I got my interview with Sra. Vargas. In fact, her daughter, Alzirinha, arranged the meeting with her mother, after I reached her by phone to request assistance. She was a good friend of a number of my new acquaintances, so I had simply phoned her to see whether she might be willing to help me do the interview. Sra. Vargas was an amiable and gracious lady, without airs, and easy to talk to. Alzirinha served as interpreter, since my broken and very limited Portuguese was inadequate.

Other freelance pieces that I handled included the huge engineering project of draining the Baixada Fluminense in the state of Rio de Janeiro. The marsh drainage story involved foot-leather reporting in the hot summer sun and produced a good environmental story along with a map.

I also conducted an interview (at the suggestion of the U.S. Embassy) with Sra. Lourival Fontes, wife of Brazil's information and propaganda chief. Sra. Fontes, it was thought, was pro-American and loved our high fashion magazines. My interview with Sra. Fontes was something else! It was conducted in three languages: French, Portuguese, and English. Sra. Fontes neither understood nor spoke any English, and my Portuguese was fragmentary, to say the least. So I tried my best with wobbly French and some basic French-Latin words with Portuguese endings. I took notes in English. It was the most exhausting interview I've ever done.

Brazil was the only country in which I attempted to do reporting or send anything back to the *Times*, but my stretch there was too short to write anything political. However, my stay in Brazil was still a daily display of new experiences and pleasures. There were days on the glorious beaches, playing handball or swimming a bit and then dozing in the sun, despite the heat. I ended up with such a deep tan (and naturally bleached hair) that my normal appearance didn't return for a year. I also visited one or two of several local casinos—very gala, crowded, and fascinating to watch, but without personal temptation to gamble. There was the whole explosion of color, activity, music, dancing, and feasting during the famous Carnival. In Rio, this was a four-day event when the public areas all over the city filled with crowds from the *favellas*, all shooting at nearby observers with the ubiquitous perfume guns. At times I felt overwhelmed, but it was all fun, exhilarating, and exhausting. On normal days, Harry Bagley and other friends showed us around the colonial parts of Rio and taught me a little about the Portuguese history of this enormous area. One evening, he even took me on a stroll through Rio's red-light district—another "first" in my collection of unusual experiences.

One of my favorite stories from the trip involves a weekend that Jean and I spent in Salvador, in Bahia, to visit friends we had made in our first hotel. When we arrived back at the Rio airport, I was surprised to find both Frank and Harry waiting for me. They both had somber expressions and sadly asked, "Has someone in your family been very ill? Or died? An uncle maybe?" "No," I replied, puzzled. Finally, Harry showed me a cable. FRANK GAR RIO NONA UNCLE, it read. The two men had been bugging Western Union for two days for the "missing words"! I burst out with a big laugh. "It's cablese," I blurted out. "It says simply that my sister has had a baby boy!"

Jean and I also flew to São Paulo for a couple of days to see the big city. The most interesting leg of that junket was the flight back to Rio. We had to wait at the airport for a couple of hours that morning while repairs were made to the engine of the plane, an old German-built aircraft for which no spare parts were available because of the war. Finally, without any testing, the craft rolled up to the gate and collected its passengers. All the way back to Rio I felt sure the plane would fall apart, and then upon landing at Rio's risky airfield, it came in at such an angle from the mountains that the plane tilted seriously to the left. Out my window I could see gravel and stones flowing through the wing flaps, then the plane steadied and we landed safely. I was just plain wobbly for the next hour.

Our lovely apartment, near Copacabana beach, had become a modest social center, maybe because we had air conditioning (I think) and a good cook in the kitchen. John Gunther came by one evening while on a fact-finding tour for his book in Brazil, and so did a Newport philanthropist and lawn-tennis supporter, who brought two tennis stars whom he was escorting on a South American trip. Later I drove with them up to Petrópolis for a sightseeing visit.

Best of all, we were able to host our own dinner party for six friends with a traditional Brazilian dish, *feijoada*. This is a wonderful concoction of dried pork (bits from each part of the pig), rice, black beans, cornmeal, and seasonings, all made at home by Marika, the family cook, and served with *cachaça* (sugar cane brandy). We all ate and drank until sated, and then fell asleep.

After three months, it was time to move on. The last leg of our trip from New York on the Grace Line would take us to Buenos Aires, with quick stops at Santos, the great coffee export center, and Montevideo, Uruguay. Buenos Aires had a true "big city" aura: lively and colorful and very Spanish. We soon learned that Argentine Spanish is different: elsewhere the *ll* is usually a liquid sound, but in Argentina it has a soft *sh* sound. Jean and I learned this when we went to visit an acquaintance from the ship, Maria Castellano. The doorman in her apartment building denied she lived there until we remembered how to pronounce that *ll*.

Arnaldo Cortesi, a well-known *Times* correspondent, had been evacuated from his longtime post in Rome and reassigned to Buenos Aires. He was very debonair and courteous, taking us both out for martini and beefsteak dinners a couple of times. Otherwise I have very few memories of doing much sightseeing or interviewing in Buenos Aires. I knew I would be there too short a time to learn and write about anything, so I suppose Jean and I generally just enjoyed the beef and the special broth called *jugo de carne.*

Our departure from Argentina was much more dramatic. We were ticketed to fly directly across the Andes to Santiago, Chile. Our plane landed first at Córdoba, just before the Andes' peaks rose up. A bad storm was raging in the pass that was usually used by passenger planes, so we waited overnight in Córdoba. The next morning, the Aconcagua Pass was still closed, so our plane, an old DC-3, took off on a more southern route, flying high (about 16,000 feet) with only rickety individual tubes of oxygen hanging from the cabin ceiling. I got a severe headache and Jean an upset stomach, but we were both basically okay upon arrival.

The *New York Times* correspondent Carlos Phillips greeted me very cheerfully and suggested I meet with a Chilean English-language magazine editor who focused on inter-American topics. This man, Carlos De Vidts, became a good friend over many years. He and his wife entertained us in their home, where we met all his children and really appreciated this look at Chilean private life. The long-time American Ambassador Claude Bowers was equally sociable and entertained us nicely.

Travel to see anything outside the city was impractical, as was often true in most of the capitals we visited. Carlos drove us to see Valparaiso, the huge port city, but other sightseeing was out of reach. But we did meet other young journalists, all eager to practice their English and find out how I got my job. (As far as I could tell, there were no female journalists working for newspapers or wire services anywhere in South America. I also learned I had to use the courtesy title "doctora" to introduce myself.)

The trip to Peru turned out to be unexpectedly rich in experiences and education. Travel up the west coast of South America was, again, by Grace Line steamer, first from Valparaiso to the port of Lima and then home via the Panama Canal. There was no resident *New York Times* correspondent in Lima, so I turned to the U.S. Embassy for suggestions of places and people to see. At a social gathering there, I met the wife of an embassy officer (I have forgotten her name, alas) who befriended me and arranged two of the most interesting and educational events of my whole trip.

She asked if I would like to see a special school for children from the illiterate slums of Lima; she volunteered at the school and thought it was making a difference. "Yes, of course," I replied eagerly, and so Jean and I went with her on a typically gray day to the school, well away from the grandeur of the national government. I was escorted from one classroom to another, all filled with excited youngsters, and I was introduced as a journalist from the land of the sun. With my blond hair, blue eyes, and—unusual to them—5'7" height, I was instantly a sensation; youngsters fingered my clothing and reached for my hands to make sure I was real. They had never seen anyone like me! At the end of the tour, I was presented with a batch of childish drawings of myself: a yellow-haired goddess from the sunny realm up north. I was overwhelmed by their excitement and saw how alien we North Americans were to this Andean-Hispanic world. I wished I could have stayed in Lima long enough to do a story about this school and the good work it was doing.

I mentioned to my hostess that I'd love to find a way to get up into the Andes—Lima then had no tourist services—and she turned up with a plan: her husband and a fellow Rotarian, a Peruvian lawyer, were planning a fishing trip for that weekend and could give us a ride to Huancayo, a then small town near their fishing spot. So, off we went, with the lawyer driving and explaining our surroundings. When we reached 16,000 feet, the high point on this road, he stopped to let us get out and experience walking a bit in such thin air. It was eerie—sort of like trying to walk on eggshells.

Then we drove down to Huancayo, at 12,000 feet a dusty collection of small, stucco-type business buildings and nearby homes. The hotel was on the second floor of a restaurant, facing the central square. Accommodations were simple, clean, comfortable, and modern. We ate quickly and then went to bed. The next morning, the square began to fill with the regular Saturday market. Soon, Andean peasant women and men congregated in a whirl of bright colors and the buzz of native speech. Typical Andean hats—large-brimmed and with boxy heads—were everywhere. We roamed about—there were no trinkets for tourists—and as we ambled back toward the hotel, we were suddenly confronted by our driver, who said the men had decided to skip their fishing plan. Our driver was a well-known Rotarian in Lima and the local Rotary chief apparently wanted him to stay for a visit.

The local Rotary Club planned a reception for their dignified visitors from Lima, including us. The party took place in the restaurant, which had been cleared of tables and furnished with semicircle of dining chairs that were occupied by the wives of the Huancayo Rotary Club. Jean and I were seated with them. After a few minutes of introduction (of the men, not us) a waiter with a tray of shot glasses began circling the ladies and offering pisco sours to the wives and their husbands standing behind them. Jean and I politely accepted this ritual offering, which was very good. The performance was then repeated twice! I guess the local guests were accustomed to this, but three pisco sours at midday, at 12,000 feet, was too much for Jean and me! We both ate a little of the spaghetti lunch that was served and then went to bed for a long nap. Thus did I learn to be very wary of pisco sours.

Later that afternoon, our companions reappeared to drive us to see a nearby Carnegie equatorial research station, a shining spot of ultramodern technical equipment in the midst of grain fields where women were threshing wheat by hand. This scene, it seemed to me, was the perfect metaphor for the economics of South America: modernity and sophistication at the top of society and back-breaking workers and illiterates at the bottom. There was no middle class.

A couple of days later, we were back on our Grace Liner, heading north with quick pauses at ports in Ecuador and Colombia, where local vendors swarmed around the ship and offered the most exquisite panama hats for a few dollars apiece. Then we sailed through the Panama Canal and its wondrous system of locks and spent the final week cruising through the Caribbean to New York. I was back home by mid-July 1941.

My unusual travel fellowship did not require any kind of written report to the journalism school, but I went to see Dean Ackerman, anyway. My nine months in a world of different languages and customs certainly taught me adaptability in and acceptance of other cultures. It also gave me self-confidence in many new social settings, such as an international cruise ship. Dean Ackerman was pleased that I had a few stories from Brazil published in the *Times* and that as a J-school scholar I was readily accepted at the professional level by officials of all countries. He laughed when I told him that in Brazil I was called *Doctora* Baldwin—the only conceivable title for a woman of my qualifications. I told the dean that I couldn't see any special direct results of Roosevelt's Good Neighbor Policy for South America, but the people were generally very friendly and pleased to see a North American visitor. I have kept a special eye on South America—and the world at large—ever since.

CHAPTER 3

*C*areer and Marriage

In the five years following my 1939 graduation from Vassar, I whirled through an extraordinary upward spiral fueled by luck, unexpected opportunities, and I suppose my own increasing skills and social sophistication. I didn't know just where I was heading—in fact, I was just learning the true meaning of good journalism—but a hire by *The New York Times* was an achievement I couldn't have dreamed up for myself. I was—as I see now—a very early beneficiary of the slow shift of women into the men's working world. I was a feminist pioneer without quite realizing it.

After my return from South America, I spent a few weeks reorienting myself to ordinary life and visiting my parents at the beach in New Jersey before I returned to work. Walking into that big metro newsroom was sort of like returning home, but with one change: there was another young woman reporter on the staff! I was back at my old desk, next to Kathleen McLaughlin. I also got to know a couple of the women who worked in an office separate from the main news operations and covered such "women's news" as women's club activities and charity events. One from this group—Adelaide Handy—and I became friends and ultimately rented a furnished apartment together on East 44th Street. The United Nations now dominates this area, but in the 1940s (I was told years later) the Beaux-Arts apartments were well known for its singles bar (which I never noticed) and social accommodations.

Only a few assignments from that autumn stick in my memory, but I recall those vividly. One day I was sent to New Haven to cover the arrival of a contingent of English schoolchildren sent to America to escape the bombing of London. This was to be the top "human interest" story of the day, but it was ruined by measles: the whole train full of youngsters was quarantined by an outbreak of the disease, so no one could greet them, no reporters could interview any of them, and the children were immediately whisked away to a private sanctuary. The result, of course, was not much of a story. I raced to the only Western Union operator at the railroad station, who moved my piece to New York immediately—and left one of New York's best-known tabloid feature writers (maybe Dorothy Kilgallen) fuming at the telegrapher.

And there was the one assignment, seemingly innocuous, that became a major event for me: a Plaza Hotel banquet at which Mayor Fiorello LaGuardia was to speak. Before I reached the Plaza that Saturday night, I read some of the advance material I received about this annual event of the St. Nicholas Society, an honored historic group stemming from the early Dutch settlers on Manhattan Island. A close reading of the information led me to suspect that this was a stag dinner. "Keep going," I muttered to myself as I went on up to the Plaza ballroom, which was indeed full of men in formal evening attire.

I quickly moved to the side chairs, where two male reporters, from the *New York Herald Tribune* and *City News Service,* were waiting. We knew one another, so we chatted and wondered what would transpire for me. Finally, a very courteous gentleman approached and said, "Excuse me, ma'am, but I'm afraid you are in the wrong place." I quickly identified myself and explained that I was there to work, not as a guest. "Well," said the gentleman, "please come with me to tell the Grand Marshall for the event."

And so I met a picturesque gentleman with a white goatee and a broad orange band across his jacket. He repeated that I was in the wrong place. "Ladies are not invited to our banquets," he explained.

"I'm sorry, sir," I replied. "I understand what you are saying, but I am not here as a lady. I am a reporter for *The New York Times* and was assigned by my editor to cover Mayor LaGuardia."

The gentlemen blinked a moment. "Very well. If you will wait until the members make their ceremonial entrance into the dining room, you may join the press table." I thanked him and quietly joined my two press colleagues, who had already started nipping at the large bottle of Scotch on the dining table. I did not drink any; this was a working dinner, and

I managed to keep the other two from quarreling over some Anglo-Irish political issue. The dinner was ordinary and so was LaGuardia's speech—hence no story for the paper, when I called in to dictate at about 10 p.m.

I should mention that, among the 150 or so tuxedoed guests, only one knew me: the lawn tennis promoter who had visited my apartment one evening in Rio. He came over to say hello, and later, after I had been cleared to stay, he offered me a drink but disappeared into the mob at the bar. However, another nearby gentleman handed me a shot of whiskey. I took a tiny sip.

Three years later I learned who this Samaritan was: my new husband, Clinton Brown! I truly didn't recall him from that bowtie crowd, but his own memory was clear. Later, when his father expressed continuing doubt about my having been at that famous stag dinner, we proved it by producing the special party gift from that night: identical souvenir decanters emblazoned with the St. Nicholas Society emblem.

The next day was December 7.

I went to work as usual, enjoyed lunch out with some colleagues, and came back to the office to hear the bellowing voice of a senior reporter who was bending over a newfangled device called a teletype machine. He shouted, "This machine is crazy. It is saying something about a bombing attack at Pearl Harbor!" For a moment he believed that the teletype was wild.

Instantly, the whole office sprang to life: phones rang, editors gave orders, staff reporters were called in, senior *Times* management appeared, and the new, tense rhythms of war reporting began. I was assigned to some event totally irrelevant to the big news, and by late afternoon I returned to the office. On the shuttle I bumped into Barney Darnton, one of the paper's best-known reporters, who looked unkempt and annoyed. He had been called in from his home in Connecticut but didn't know why. I told him. Barney was shipped out to Pearl Harbor that night and stayed with the armed forces as they came face to face with the Japanese forces. Killed in combat only a few months later, he was the first newspaper victim of the war.

The flow of work in the newsroom proceeded more or less normally, but coverage changed, as everything was now related to the war in some way: speeches, fundraising for troops or Bundles for Britain, increases in draft calls, impact on the economy, reports from the Pacific combat area, and the activation of army and navy reservists. Everyone's outlook, personal and political, was totally reoriented. I don't recall any particular stories I covered, but I handled my share of charity fundraisers and other local events.

Then, in January, Assistant Managing Editor Bruce Rae called me to his desk. He explained that Arthur Krock, the chief Washington correspondent—head of the Washington bureau of the *Times*—would like me to move to the Washington bureau to cover "women's news and consumer news." I hardly believed my ears. This was the most prestigious job I could imagine: a Washington correspondent for *The New York Times,* and an increase in pay to $55 a week! I was ecstatic and moved as quickly as I could to Washington. Before the end of January, I had disentangled myself from the Beaux-Arts apartment and began to search for a place to live. Washington was swarming with new federal employees, new soldiers and sailors, and thousands of top career people from the academic and business worlds seeking to serve the nation. All normal rental space—hotels, rooming houses, or apartments—were full. After bouncing around for a while, I was offered a Connecticut Avenue sublet to share with another newcomer. This was a godsend; I lived in that apartment in Cathedral Mansions, with some changes of roommates, until 1944.

The Washington bureau of *The New York Times* was then—and still is—a major center for reporting and writing about all aspects of national news. Our boss, Arthur Krock—always known as Mr. Krock—presided over a staff of perhaps fifty people: reporters, editors, telegraphers (old-fashioned Morse code experts), librarians, photographers, and secretarial help. Most impressively, our space—the seventh floor of the Albee Building—was air conditioned! Also, we had our own "morgue": a research library filled with reference books and decades of itemized clippings from the *Times*. As far as I know, I was the first woman reporter assigned to the bureau. But a lovely old lady named Winifred Mallon had a small desk there and appeared only occasionally; she handled diplomatic and social news and, notably, Mrs. Roosevelt's press conferences. (Men were not permitted at Mrs. Roosevelt's sessions.) Many years later I learned that Winnie was not a staff reporter but a space writer—that is, she was paid by the inch for occasional stories somehow not quite worthy of full staff coverage.

As quickly as I could, I settled into the job. Most of my time was spent at the Office of Price Administration or at the War Production Board, covering the steady stream of orders affecting the economy: rations, shortages of consumer goods, new limits on all kinds of consumer goods and foods, and price controls on many basic consumer items. And on the Hill, legislation began moving through Congress to permit women to serve in the military. The army had begun accepting women in an auxiliary status in 1941 (later changed to regular status) and in that spring of 1942, legislation to admit women to the regular U.S. Naval Reserve became law. All of this was on my beat, so I soon learned my way around Congress and the offices of the political and government men involved in this "dangerous" experiment. I also ended up doing a modest amount of economic reporting: the impact of the OPA and WPB was enormous.

I loved it all. I was busy, met lots of new people, and enjoyed a special respect in semi-official Washington because my gender made me a novelty. There was a strong cadre of women reporters in Washington then, but none doing daily reporting for a major daily newspaper. I got along well with—and truly liked—most of these experienced older women: May Craig, Esther Van Wagoner Tufty, Doris Fleeson, Bess Furman (who later moved to the *Times*), and Emma Bugbee, to name a few. But I suppose I mystified them in a way, since I was just twenty-three at the time. One of them even asked me directly whether I'd landed my job by sleeping with the managing editor—or maybe the publisher!

The truth is that Mr. Krock, whom I had met a couple of times, was always pleasant to me but paid me no special attention and always called me *Miss Baldwin*. Several of the men at the bureau kept a distasteful distance from me, but most were helpful and friendly. I also got to know the telegraphers quite well—a trio of former railroad telegraphers who seemed to breathe the Morse code. When it was my turn to stay in the office until 11 p.m. closing, I kibitzed on their poker games and heard some colorful tales.

That summer I went to Mexico for my vacation, to show off my independence and relative affluence, I guess. My plan was to fly to San Antonio and then take a bus or train to Mexico City. A friend of Mr. Krock was on that plane, as was the new *New York Times* correspondent for Mexico City. "Don't you dare take a bus to Mexico City," declared Mr. Krock's friend. "I'll drive you down," said the new *Times* man. After checking with the mother of a friend in San Antonio, who agreed that the bus idea was dangerous, I decided not to let my rather prudish social attitudes spoil a wonderful offer. A few days later, Camille Cianfarra and I took off to Mexico City in an old used car with four old used tires, which the *Times* purchased for him.

The first tire blew out about halfway to Laredo, and the so-called spare then helped us get there. Cian wanted to cross the river into Mexico, where new rubber tires were readily available, so we navigated into Nuevo Juárez, put the car in a garage, and picked it up in the morning with two new tires. This carried us as far as San Luis Potosí, where the electrical system conked out. I was driving at that point, and I had to keep driving behind another car, dependent on its headlights, for about twenty miles—a blinding experience! We got the car repaired and arrived in Mexico City the next day. I enjoyed a lovely two weeks there, and most significantly, I met Sally Reston, wife of Scotty Reston, an outstanding journalist in the London bureau of the *Times* (and later managing editor). Sally and I remained good friends for many years, as did Scotty and I.

Back at work, Luther Huston, the editor for the Washington bureau, meted out my daily assignments. I began to develop new friendships and thoroughly enjoyed my time off on weekends. Then, in October, I received another surprising phone call. I was at my desk and the caller quickly identified herself: "This is Mildred McAfee calling." She had just been named by the U.S. Navy to oversee introducing women into the navy. There would be no separate corps for women, so they had to be meshed into the navy wherever needed, either individually or in small groups after completing training courses. Captain McAfee's job was to help pinpoint where these new sailors would go.

"Miss Baldwin," she asked me, "would you consider accepting a commission in the navy to work in the navy press office and handle news concerning this whole program?"

That was a jolt—and not a very welcome one. My current job was much too exciting and important to me; why should I give it up? On the other hand, was it fair to say no when no man in the United States was allowed that choice? After a weekend of discussing the issue with friends and family, I decided that, in my conscience, there really wasn't any choice: I had to accept the navy's offer.

The commissioning process began immediately, starting with the mandatory physical exam. This was a laugh. The navy recruiting office, just a few steps away from the *Times* bureau, was a busy place, with a full roster of doctors and medics to process newcomers, but I posed a problem. All their medical exam papers were for men. After considerable tittering and chuckling, the form was adapted somehow and I was cleared. On October 14, I received my ensign's commission and moved my workplace to the zero wing of the navy department's ancient building at 17th Street and Constitution Avenue. For one month, I attended a special officer training school at Smith College. From there I returned in full uniform (that Mainbocher-designed uniform that was so popular), ready to work.

Nona in navy uniform, 1943

Navy press was the source of all official navy press releases and the required channel for all journalists to see anyone in the building. It was a hectic spot, open every hour of every day, but really not an exciting place to work. All major navy combat news came from the high command in the Pacific; we handled the hometown stories of battle casualties, occasional policy statements, and all press inquiries

There was some confusion about what to call us female newcomers. Officially we were simply Reservists or Women Reserves, but the nickname WAVES soon took hold. Based on a carefully drawn Navy regulation phrase (Women Accepted for Voluntary Emergency Service), many people still believe the WAVES formed a separate corps with its own military chain of command. Not so: my boss was Captain Leon Lovett, USN, Director of Public Relations.

For the next two years, work in the navy press office was routine and—as a reporter—not very challenging. One day I was sent as the navy representative to a presidential press conference in FDR's office. The usual small herd of big-name newspaper reporters moved into the Oval Office, and the president sat at his desk, chatting with staff or friends. I was, I think, the only woman present. I received nods from acquaintances, quizzical looks from others, and a questioning look from FDR himself. Someone explained my uniformed presence, and FDR turned to me, nodded, and turned back to the waiting reporters. And that was my moment with FDR.

Another time I covered a press conference by Henry Stimson, secretary of war, at the Pentagon. These major events always drew the top correspondents in the country for an official update on the war. Hanson Baldwin, senior military correspondent for *The New York Times*, was there, and he greeted me with his usual sarcastic banality: "Hello, Nona, what are you doing here? Why don't you go back to the kitchen where you belong?" I laughed, of course—and so did Hanson. Because we had the same family name, though we were in no way related, we had always bantered, but invariably with a slight edge of seniority in his words. Later, the day after the D-Day invasion, Hanson tried to send news of my new husband's survival by slipping Clint's name into his lead story from the Navy Command Center off Omaha Beach. The copy desk in New York failed to recognize the personal message; Hanson told Clinton about it months later. After the war ended, Clint and I had very friendly contacts with Hanson, and I actually cooked a dinner at home for him. (He never did like letting women join the navy.)

While my day job was rather tedious, my social life was active. Washington was overflowing with young navy and army officers looking for dates. Tony and Fay Leviero became very close friends of mine (I had known Tony at the *Times* before he went into uniform in 1941) and entertained me with their friends. Somehow I got to know several young Washington socialites, including Kathleen Kennedy, and attended concerts or picnics and small parties with them. Beer was always available, but there was only one hard liquor for social drinking: cheap and raw rye whiskey.

I especially enjoyed resuming contact with Jim Tobin, whom I had met originally on the SS *Washington* in 1939. Jim was involved in government economic operations and lived with three other Harvard guys in a house on Reservoir Road. That group gave great Saturday evening parties! In addition to these casual parties on Reservoir Road, I had a full calendar of other social activities.

On one evening in February 1944, I had a blind date in a small group to attend a National Symphony Orchestra concert. After the concert, we all walked from Constitution Hall to the Arts Club for a quick drink before heading home. We all sat down at a table with Hans Kindler, then director of the NSO, and were quietly singing along with a piano player whose repertoire drew from old barbershop songbooks. That kind of music always set my feet tapping and broke out my humming voice. I wandered over to join the group of singers right by the piano. Suddenly someone grabbed my left arm and loudly announced, "She's a JG and, by God, she's pretty!" (My navy uniform had 1½ sleeve stripes, representing my rank of lieutenant junior grade.) I turned immediately to slap and shake off the offending boor when I saw on his sleeve the 2½ stripes of a lieutenant commander! He was obviously rather drunk, but it still seemed unwise to strike a more senior officer. He did pull back but clearly wanted to take me with him to another party. I declined very firmly but told him that he could reach me the next morning at navy press, where I would be on duty. He told me his name—Clinton Brown—and I returned home by bus with my blind date, whom I never saw again.

I was at my duty post by 8:00 the next morning and all was quiet. Then came his phone call, apologizing for his rudeness and asking me out for lunch. Since I couldn't leave my job until 4 p.m. he joined me in the navy cafeteria. He was sober, handsome, interesting to talk to, and a Yale graduate with a law degree, so he was certainly someone special. I asked him to accompany me on a prearranged visit to see a friend's new baby, and then we went out to dinner at a French restaurant near the Shoreham. I knew that I had met someone who would be very important to me.

Clint was stationed at Solomons Island, preparing his group of LCIs (Landing Craft Infantry) to cross the Atlantic for action in Europe. He returned to Washington on the following weekend, when he asked if I would come to New York to see him on the weekend of March 24. That would be his last chance to see me before shipping out in early April, and he felt obliged to visit his parents, too, who lived in New York City.

Clint met me at Penn Station, registered me at the Hotel Gotham, and then took me to meet an old friend of his, Radford Bascome, at a private party. Then the four of us—Rad, his date, Clinton, and I—moved on to the Stork Club, then the epitome of New York nightclubs. This was a pretty heady, rather glamorous scene for me and I was having great fun. Clint took me onto the dance floor. He loved to dance! The music was romantic, and as we danced Clinton suddenly asked me to marry him. I accepted. Then we went back to the table and told Rad and his date, Helen, the news. They approved! A natural promoter, Rad then proposed that we get married right away! He knew how to get the paperwork from City Hall, and the navy headquarters at 90 Church Street could provide personal clearances (including the Wassermann test for syphilis), and we could have the ceremony at City Hall, if we wanted. Well, Rad did everything he promised. Clinton informed his parents at around 7 a.m., I believe, and, while shocked and unhappy, his parents were wonderful. Sometime during the morning, I phoned my parents in Red Bank—to be greeted with an angry outburst from my father. After several minutes of uncomplimentary aspersions, I was able to explain and he was able to tell me that Mother had fallen and was recovering from a concussion. I was embarrassed and apologetic, but I was not about to stop my wedding. He finally agreed to come to New York for the ceremony that evening. Bless him, he also called my sister at her home near New Brunswick and my brother, who was in a naval officer training program at Stevens Institute.

The marriage took place at the Church of the Transfiguration, the Browns' long-time parish church in New York City, at 8 p.m. on March 25, 1944, followed by a small reception at the St. Regis Hotel. We were both in uniform, of course. Rad was the best man for Clint, and my sister, Betty, was my maid of honor. The guest list also included approximately a dozen members of the Brown family and, arriving from various points in New Jersey, my trio of Baldwins.

There was only one momentary glitch in this remarkably smooth scenario: right before the ceremony, Father Randolph Ray called me to his office to obtain the essential information for a marriage certificate. He asked, "What is your full name? Date and place of birth? Date of baptism?" Whoops.

"I'm sorry, Father Ray, but I have never been baptized," I replied, and then realized this was no small matter in the Episcopal Church. "Father Ray, I'm a Quaker."

His face relaxed. "Do you belong to an organized meeting?" he asked.

When I responded, "Yes, the Montclair Monthly Meeting in Montclair, New Jersey," he smiled, made a couple of notes, and then went on with the paperwork—and with the marriage, thank goodness!

Newlyweds Nona Baldwin Brown and Clinton Brown, 1944

The next day, we took a quick train trip to Red Bank, New Jersey, to see Mother. Dad was still furious with me for pulling a stunt like a wedding without knowing about Mother's bedridden condition. She was actually very cheerful and welcoming, and she ended up liking Clint very much.

Of course, we both had to be at our respective duty stations on Monday morning, so somehow we booked a flight that dropped me at National Airport and took him to the big navy base at Norfolk. Before my return I had phoned one of my housemates, Mary Pauline Perry, so when I walked into my apartment that evening there was a lot of whoop-dee-doo, but I was too tired to laugh at the new-bride jokes and soon fell asleep.

On Monday morning, I reported my change of status to Captain Lovett, who immediately asked how soon my new husband would be sailing across to England. "Very early in April," I replied. Captain Lovett then issued an order giving me leave to go to Norfolk and stay until Clint's departure. So that was our "first" honeymoon: five days at the Naval Operating Base while he prepared for departure on April 3. Clinton was in command of a flotilla of ten landing craft too small to cross the Atlantic, but they did, anyway. The visit was wonderful and without tension, despite knowing the dangers ahead for him.

Clint sailed and all was quiet, except for his letters. They arrived frequently after he reached England, and they were all very long, cheerful, and emotional. I began to wonder where we would live whenever he got home. The national nervousness in anticipation of D-Day was palpable; my personal anxiety zoomed on June 6 and for the next two days until he was able to send me a cable. After he returned home in October, Clint didn't talk much about his experiences, a common reaction among veterans of major war events. Only after he died in 1996 did I learn of his D-Day experience, in the form of a long memo he wrote to himself, for no other eyes to see, the night after the battle. This unique sixty-page account of the D-Day landing now belongs to the Naval History & Heritage Command and is on file at the Washington Navy Yard.

Clinton finally came home in October and was assigned to duty at the Navy Department. We happily got reacquainted, so to speak. After several weeks of temporary housing in hotels and borrowed apartments, we finally found a simple one-bedroom apartment in Alexandria, hastily gathered some furniture, and made our first home. Clint owned a venerable two-door Studebaker, which gave us a little leeway for visiting and pleasure, but gas rationing was so low and our car so ancient that we didn't go far. Clint had been assigned to the Bureau of Ships, located near my job in the zero wing of Main Navy.

In early 1945, after many months of complaining about severe stress headaches, the navy ordered a complete physical checkup for me, which concluded that essentially I was frustrated by my dull, dead-end job. I had neither expected nor wanted this conclusion. This led to my early retirement in the summer of 1945, just as World War II was winding down. Because of his long service—active duty starting in 1941 and service in battles in the Pacific, Atlantic, and Normandy—Clint was released by the navy in October 1945.

We both looked around and decided to stay in Washington. My job at the *Times* was guaranteed because of my status as a veteran. Clint soon found work in a temporary government agency and finally wound up on Capitol Hill as a staff lawyer for the House Armed Services Committee and I returned to work in a new position at the *Times*: assistant to the Washington Sunday editor. This meant working for the special Sunday sections of the paper, mostly the Magazine and the Review of the Week. It was a great job, since I dealt with all aspects of national news, from magazine articles to weekend analytical pieces on top national news issues, plus I gathered information for economic charts and colorful anecdotes from congressional hearings. Best of all, it was a 10 a.m. to 6 p.m. job, so the working hours fit well with Clinton's.

We soon moved from Alexandria to a colorful and truly old (1815) Georgetown house. The location was wonderful, the plumbing antiquated, the kitchen too small and scruffy, and, of course, the house boasted a wobbly heating system and no air conditioning. No matter! We loved it and lived there for six years. And despite our relative poverty, we entertained quite often.

Our next-door neighbors, Bill and Virginia Shepherd, introduced us to older, socially prominent people (some of whom Clinton knew through his family and their long-standing position in the New York Social Register) who became real friends of ours. These connections continued even after Virginia died and Bill married the very sociable widow of a top American diplomat and ended only when the Shepherds were killed in an automobile accident in 1960. These social friendships persevered, most notably with Mrs. Kingdon Gould. Clinton had known her daughters—Sylvia and Edith especially—from their New York debutante days. To this day, the younger Kingdon Gould family, despite alterations in its composition, has remained close to me. I am godmother to one of their sons.

Some of my work for the paper put me in touch with diplomatic press relations officers, and this led to another facet of our social life, especially with friends in the Turkish and Indian embassies. I remember several Indian diplomatic parties where I met Mme. Pandit, Nehru's sister. I particularly recall one event when, after the formalities were concluded, the partygoers retired to the home of the Indian press attaché, Shiv Shastri, for coffee and scrambled eggs. Shiv became a good friend, staying overnight with us when he was at the UN and playing a lovely passage from a Beethoven violin concerto on Clint's old violin. Later, Shiv returned to Delhi and became a recluse. Clint and I last saw him in New Delhi in 1980.

The Turkish press attaché, Nuzhet Baba, was a very informal, affable guy who had been with Ataturk during the founding of modern Turkey, so he shared many stories about the famous Turkish president. Nuzhet liked to entertain diplomatic press reporters at his home in Chevy Chase, with his wife and some of her friends. They prepared a superb walnut chicken and rice dish offered buffet style, and we all sat around his big front porch, chatting occasionally with neighbors passing on the sidewalk.

The most surprising story from this period grew out of my work and led to a prized Baldwin family possession. In the late 1940s, the Marine Corps was pressing for money to create a memorial with a center sculpture based on the famous flag-raising at Iwo Jima. I covered this in a short magazine piece focused on the sculptor, Felix de Weldon, and his work in progress. Naturally he and I engaged in several conversations, and then one day Felix turned and asked me to sit for him. What a flattering idea! I thanked him but said I couldn't possibly afford it. I finally agreed after he made clear there would be no charge; it would be his pleasure, he said. I sat for him during at least a dozen early morning sessions in his old studio heated by a Franklin stove. Months passed before the clay model was finished and even more months before Felix could cast the bust in powdered stone. I was amazed and delighted. To thank him, I threw Felix a party at home to which I invited several important public and press figures I knew, including John R. Steelman, special assistant to President Truman. Among family and friends, the cheerful gala is usually called the "unveiling of Nona's bust."

Nona sitting for sculptor Felix de Weldon, circa 1950

In 1952, the owner of 1513 33rd Street decided to sell the Georgetown property and offered it to us for the "bargain" price of $28,000. We simply couldn't afford it, knowing full well how much modernization and renovation it required—maybe $100,000 to $200,000, we naïvely thought. Anyway, we gave it up and purchased for $20,500 a very practical, 1917 semi-detached brick house in Chevy Chase with an excellent kitchen, four bedrooms, two baths, and everything in working condition. Our new neighborhood was not socially glamorous like Georgetown, but the commute downtown was a breeze for both of us. Our new neighbors were the quintessential Washington mix of lawyers, bureaucrats, foreign service families, and journalists. We lived there happily for eleven years and owned it as a rental property until 1976. It turned out to be the wisest investment we could have made: we sold it in 1976 for $37,500!

In 1949, we finally had our "real" honeymoon: a trip to England and France on the new SS *America*. As a journalist, I suspect I received some special attention, and I eventually wrote a piece for the paper about John Locke, chief purser and very colorful career man. Then, upon landing in rationed, subdued England, we were affected immediately when our guaranteed accommodations in London that night had been rented to

47

someone else because we didn't arrive until 9 p.m. No other hotel room was available, so the *Times*'s bureau chief, Ray Daniell—who had made that reservation—put us up on sofas in his apartment. Ray and his wife were wonderfully hospitable. Plenty of unrationed Scotch whiskey helped drown Ray's fury at the hotel as well as cheer us up after a long, long day.

With heavy pressure from him, the hotel returned our room to us the next day, but we shortly left London to stay with friends Kakki and Rod Harman and family in nearby Surrey. We turned our temporary visitor's ration card over to Kakki, who promptly used this rare extra purchasing power to buy a "joint" of lamb, her first such indulgence since she and Rod had returned from Washington two years earlier. As tourists with dollars to spend, we were also issued gas coupons and were able to rent a car. With that luxury, we piled all the Harmans (two adults and two children) plus Clinton and me into an Austin Mini and drove to the beach at West Wittering for a picnic. The children were ecstatic. Then, a couple of days later, we took off on our own, tooting our way to Worcester and Bath. (There were so few cars on the roads at that time that we all tooted greetings as we passed.) Our sightseeing was quite perfunctory and included some odd moments, such as asking a bartender in the only hotel then functioning in Bath for two dry martinis. The bartender offered us an Italian wine made by someone named Martini—he simply didn't understand the gin, vermouth, and ice parts of the cocktail, and had never heard of chilling such a drink. We settled for whiskey.

After a week, we crossed the Channel and stayed in a cozy little hotel near the Madeleine. Aside from basic sightseeing, we spent most of our time visiting with Clint's first cousin, Hamilton Brown. Hammy was there to procure government help to restore his parents' lovely old manor house in Brittany, which had been rendered uninhabitable by trampling German troops.

We returned home on the SS *America*, too, so we could continue our bantering with John Locke and polish off the last of the sailing-party liquor he had put away for us. We didn't go abroad again for fifteen years.

CHAPTER 4

$\mathscr{D}$iscovery and Travel

The 1950s became a period of settling into both married life and workaday realities. I was the breakfast cook, since Clint had to leave for work, generally by bus, before I did. I was due at my office by 10 a.m. and returned home at about 6:30 p.m. I hired Sadie to work at our home from noon until 8 p.m., including cooking dinner, five days a week. This major indulgence gave us the luxury of a half hour for cocktails before 7:00 dinner and gave me the freedom to keep working. A good Southern cook as well as an unusual character, Sadie was a fixture in our lives for ten years.

At about this time, Clinton left his Capitol Hill job and set himself up in private practice. He had always wanted to try practicing law by himself, so he decided to take the plunge, allowing himself three or four years to succeed. Solo private practice amounted to a high-risk, low-return occupation, so he returned to the government, this time in the Department of Justice. He remained there, in the Tax Division, until he retired in 1977.

With our workweek pattern established, we turned to other interests: Clinton to his violin and I to sewing and cooking. Clint's violin was a simple instrument his mother had found for him but for which she never provided him any lessons. He tried to teach himself. He had a good ear, patience, and high hopes of playing a little Bach and Beethoven. But tuning that violin was an endless process! George Steiner, former member of the National Symphony Orchestra and then head of the new music department at George Washington University, agreed to give him lessons, and thus began our long friendship with George and his wife. Eventually,

Clint was able to play snippets from Paganini and a Brandenburg concerto. He loved every minute of it and led me to an equally fervent love of violin music.

My cooking and dressmaking grew partly out of economic necessity: I couldn't afford the clothes that I liked, so I tried to copy them, using Simplicity patterns with good fabric. I even secured beautiful silks from Jim Thompson's shop in Bangkok for evening dresses.

Nona, aunt Esther Baldwin, and parents Helen and Thomas Baldwin outside Hotel du Pont, Wilmington, DE, on Thanksgiving Day, 1956

In the 1950s, our social life ranged from diplomatic cocktail parties and home-cooked meals to big benefit dances at the Shoreham Hotel. We became members of the Army Navy Country Club, which offered Saturday night dinner dancing and a large outdoor swimming pool for daytime pleasure. We joined with many friends and acquaintances from our navy days as well as people from the newspaper world and Capitol Hill. The rich mix of interesting people we knew included the following: in Georgetown, a bachelor household of young diplomats, one of whom became U.S. ambassador to the Soviet Union; Brice Harlow, who was on the Armed Service Committee with Clint and ultimately became the go-to man and major confidant of President Eisenhower; and Tom and Eloise Davies (Rear Admiral), who were our close friends for years, starting with the B-36 bomber controversy. And then there were our Georgetown neighbors: Bill and Romaine Shepherd, Tina Gould (Mrs. Kingdon Gould, Sr.), Senator and Mrs. Claiborne Pell, Senator and Mrs. Estes Kefauver, and Mrs. McCook Knox, who introduced me to the American Civil War as displayed in her magnificent collection of historic paintings and manuscripts that filled her house. As my social life picked up rapidly, so did my self-assurance. I could, for example, chat as easily with Vice President Alben Barkley or a Keynesian economist as with a saleswoman at the local drugstore. My education and travels gave me good subjects for conversation. Clint and I were comfortable players on the edge of the great political game, which was fun and fascinating.

In the late 1940s, I made what was, for me, a most adventurous move: I bought a small house in Virginia. New legislation gave veterans certain housing benefits, and I decided to avail myself of one. For $200 down and $100 each month for the mortgage, I became owner of a house in Pimmit Hills—strictly G.I. housing for young World War II veterans and their families—with a kitchen, living/dining room, three very small bedrooms, and one bath. I rented it to an excellent family for five years and then sold it to them for $12,000. This wasn't exactly a get-rich-quick scheme, but it did give me enough cash to repay Aunt Esther her interest-free loan for the Morrison Street purchase. The experience was also raw evidence of the bias against women in business transactions. At first, the real estate developer didn't want to sell to me, a single female veteran. His agents insisted that my husband be on the deal, but our lawyer very quickly made my veteran's rights clear. Then the mortgage company refused to grant me a mortgage unless my husband cosigned it. I finally overcame that outmoded hurdle, too. My first civil rights win!

I was happily married and had a stable job in an exciting career. I was not a sharply competitive reporter—not a "gotcha" type—and I was uncomfortable with open confrontation and anger. I never fought for personal attention or advancement, and the modern celebratory role of many of today's women newscasters still makes me shiver. The vehement, controversial aspects of the feminist movement never attracted me. I have always avoided joining advocacy organizations of any kind, whether political, economically-focused, or social; I just didn't like bearing any kind of label, which helped me to avoid charges of bias. All along I truly felt that professional competence was my strongest asset—a naïve belief, I suppose, but one that served me well for many years. In that sense, I have always been a strong feminist.

When we moved to Morrison Street in 1951, our budget was stretched. Our two incomes were modest, at perhaps $15,000 a year combined, and with mortgage payments and car insurance and such, we lived on very stringent weekly allowances. But family visitors were always welcome, and Father even managed to bring Mother down from New Jersey for a few days. She couldn't get over my form of entertainment for friends, who would come for cocktails and dinner and gossipy politics. Mother wondered why we didn't plan something special, such as bridge or charades, as after-dinner entertainment. That never occurred to me! There was always a lot to talk about in Washington, I explained, and so we entertain ourselves, with or without demitasse and liqueurs.

In my Sunday Department job, I was no longer doing daily news reporting, but I was often on Capitol Hill to cover some of the extraordinary Senate hearings of that period. Harry Truman had built his reputation with his World War II hearings on labor issues, but in the Eisenhower Administration, Congress was alive with charges and hearings involving so-called "Un-American Activities." I covered many of these, mostly seeking unusual details for the Review of the Week, from Senator Joe McCarthy's accusatory fireworks to the toxic and critical Army–McCarthy hearings, during which McCarthy accused the army leadership of what he deemed subversive behavior. Even without today's noisy cable newscasts, the whole country was roused by McCarthyism. I was on the scene when Joseph Welch, the Senate committee's prominent lawyer and interrogator, turned to McCarthy after he charged the secretary of the army with communist leanings: "Have you no sense of decency, sir, at long last? Have you left no sense of decency?" McCarthy seemed to cringe; the hearing fell silent.

I listened to many hours of debate on the floor of the House and Senate. In those days, an occasional filibuster lasted all night (Senator Wayne Morse of Oregon was especially good at this) and many politically explosive roll calls ran until 2 or 3 a.m. I became familiar with all the back stairs between Senate and House chambers and got to know many members: a favorite, Vice President Alben Barkley, liked to bestow a fatherly kiss on the foreheads of some of us bright young ladies. I handled, editorially, several articles he wrote for the Magazine, and I did an investigative piece to identify a bronze statue of a man that had been in the vice president's suite of offices for decades. I finally uncovered his obscure identity, but no one ever knew why it was in the veep's office.

Lester Markel, the Sunday editor, was always alert to weather stories—floods, drought, tornadoes, hurricanes, and extreme heat or cold—so I ended up with much weather bureau reporting. Long-range forecasting, as we now have it, was only a dream for a few meteorologists, but some advance information was being gathered by airplanes flying into the center of forming hurricanes. This exciting and dangerous stuff was good story material. I flew to Kindley Field, Bermuda, from which the Air Force weather planes flew to reach inside approaching storms; I wanted to ride into a storm to describe the experience, but both *The New York Times* and the Air Force said no. I instead interviewed pilots as they landed, and I nabbed some excellent photographs. When I flew back to New York on a Friday, Markel told me to stay in the city and write my piece immediately. Another hurricane was approaching New England and my piece was needed for the issue going to press on Monday. The pictures and short article made it to print. The following year, thanks to the friendly meteorologists I had worked with, *Nona* was added to the all-female list of hurricane names. Luckily, the hurricane season was moderate; there was no number 14.

During the 1950s and 1960s, our summer vacations were spent visiting friends and exploring nearby regions, such as the southern part of the eastern shore. Both of us enjoyed browsing in unusual places, such as isolated Tangier Island, where the locals' speech still has a cockney lilt. John and Evie Hayes's cottage on the beach at Lewes was a frequent destination for us, sometimes as guests and sometimes as chaperones for their son and his friends. This favorite refuge was a low-key spot for long walks up the beach with bay waters quietly lapping on sand and occasional chats with friends along the way. John and Evie both worked for *The Washington Post*: she a fashion editor and he a senior executive heading the *Post*'s broadcast business. Their cottage became a magnet for other press friends.

And at least once each summer we tripped north to the senior Browns' recently purchased farm in Staatsburg, New York. My father-in-law clearly hoped to make this a grand family domain, with a lovely main house, once part of a colonial tavern, plus two barns, one or two tenant houses, and a gorgeous view of the Hudson River Valley from the top of the hill. The spot was lovely, but scorching hot in the summer and incapable of producing any marketable crop except raspberries. Filling quart containers of the luscious berries from the bushes and taking them to the village store was always part of our vacation.

During those visits we met Daisy Suckley; her mother, Bessie; and two brothers, all of whom lived at Wilderstein, a decrepit yet intriguing nineteenth-century "designer" house. Now open to the public as a historic house museum in Rhinebeck, it offers a clear look at the lifestyle of the Hudson Valley aristocracy, including the Livingstons, the Roosevelts, and other old-money Americans. Daisy, the oldest daughter and longest surviving child of the Suckley family, was a wispy, quiet, and very gracious lady who, as the world now knows, was Franklin Delano Roosevelt's closest companion for the last fifteen years of his life. Daisy was so discreet that no one knew how very constant their relationship was until after she died in 1991, when executors found a suitcase full of diary entries and extensive correspondence with FDR, which was later made public. Clint and I visited Daisy many times, nibbling cheese and crackers in the kitchen or taking her to Foster's in Rhinebeck for lunch. She must have been laughing to herself at all the FDR biographers who had tried to get her to talk. Our friendship with the Suckley family continued until very recently, when one of her nieces, who lived in Annapolis, died.

Monty Anderson, Daisy Suckley, and Nona in Rhinebeck, NY, 1990

Clint, of course, was familiar with the Clinton family history, including General James Clinton of George Washington's staff; Governor

George Clinton, who fought so hard against the new federal Constitution; and Governor DeWitt Clinton, New York City mayor, father of the Erie Canal, and progenitor of many small towns across the country. All this was new to me and fed my growing interest in historic furnishings and preservation of American historic buildings.

In the late 1950s, we suffered two very sad losses: my mother in 1958 and Clinton's father in 1960. Mother had a debilitating stroke in the middle of the night and summoned help by banging on her apartment wall. She survived only a few months, leaving Father quite forlorn. He was an exceptionally self-sufficient man—he could cook meals when necessary, always purchased the groceries, and was very businesslike in managing his time, so living alone did not upset him. However, he had developed type-2 diabetes and was careless about his diet. He had a foot sore that wasn't healing, but he went off on a business trip, anyway. From the Pittsburgh airport he had to turn home immediately to Montclair and went straight to Mountainside Hospital, where he lost his left leg to gangrene. Very bravely he carried on, learned to walk with a prosthesis, and stayed in his apartment for several more years.

Father Brown's death in 1960, after a second heart attack, was a shock. His widow's response was clear and quick: after he was buried, she wanted to close the New York City apartment, which they seldom used, to save the $200 monthly rent, and then close up and sell the Staatsburg property, which was no place for her to spend the winter months alone. She wanted to move to Washington in a hurry.

These decisions presented us with a mountain of work. Mother Brown (known to all the family as *Gunga*, baby babble for "grandmother") and Ilona, her sister, were the managers. Clint and I spent half that summer packing, trashing, moving, and sweating. Clint's brother, Jim, his wife, and even the older grandchildren worked like beavers. Somehow we got Gunga into an apartment near us in Washington, on Connecticut Avenue. The 89th Street apartment was emptied immediately; the big house was virtually empty by October 1. At the end of this cascade of change, Gunga sank back into her new home with relief and contentment. Clinton's father, Pumpa, seemed a difficult man to live with, being very strict in his religious and social ideas, very precise in his calculations and manner, and seemingly immune to frivolity or humor. He and I once grappled a bit over my non-baptized condition. Pumpa contended that I simply couldn't be a Christian without baptism. "Well," I replied, "I think I'm as good a

Christian as you are—and so does Father Ray!" The subject never came up again.

My mother-in-law, whose full name was Erszebet de Vaidja Duma, was born and raised in Budapest. A petite lady who was always gracious and very hard working, she was fluent in English, French, German, and Hungarian and brought a refined European accent to the Brown-Clinton family. Everyone liked her, except her mother-in-law, Florence Bleeker Brown. "So," she was heard to say as the assembled family greeted the new bride in her home in New York, "so this is the European adventuress." Her eldest son, Clinton, had met and married her in Budapest, and I guess she never recovered from the social unorthodoxy.

Clinton and I had long since become familiar with the other Brown family issues. Clint's brother, Jim, with his wife, Polly, and children (six altogether, starting in 1948) had moved to Washington with our help around 1950. Jim had spent five years as a private in the army and had no college experience, so he faced severe employment issues. For seven years he attended college part time and worked as a research clerk for the *Chicago Tribune*'s Washington office. As their family grew, so did their housing needs until they finally settled near us in a large older house in Chevy Chase. Clint and I joined their family life as much as we could, or they wanted, as their needs were often quite pressing. Their six children are a great mainstay in my life today, especially Betsy and Lexie. Jim Brown died in 1978; his wife, Polly, in 2009. The surviving children are Betsy, Jamie, Lexie, twins David and Clinton, and Nona (called Nikki).

Because they lived just down the alley from our house on Morrison Street, the youngsters soon found their way to our back door and our excellent housekeeper, Blanche. Years later, I learned how so much of my kitchen goodies disappeared so quickly, and how fond the kids were of both our home and our cat.

By this time cats had become a fixture in our lives, starting with an episode in Georgetown when our neighbor Lee Prina accidentally hit our car while driving her cat to the vet. We then had a kitten, which Sadie, our housekeeper, loved. She told us about a friendly feline visitor who came over the fence to visit, who turned out to be Simon, the Prina's Siamese cat, always identified by Sadie as a "simonaise" cat. That laugh is still alive, seventy years later, since the Prinas, who became close friends, are now at Grand Oaks, just a few doors away from my apartment.

For years, Clint and I had cats, always black, sometimes as many as eight at one time just after a litter had been born. For a long time, Monkey was our beloved cat, and although I can't recall the exact cat-by-cat changes over the years, often with the help of Lee Prina, we ended up eventually with four: two old ladies named Lizzie and Lonce and two young ones: Cookie, the male, and Sweetie, the female. Somehow there was a happy division of feline habits, with the two old ladies living on the second and third floor of the Kanawha Street house and the two youngsters on the first floor and basement. When I was confined to bed after surgery in 1980, Lizzie was the one who always curled up with me, a nice warm ball of purring fur. Cookie, the tomcat, clearly favored Clinton, and for good reason: Cookie almost died at birth, but Clinton saved him by patiently feeding the week-old kitten with warmed dog milk in a doll's feeding bottle. Cookie, the last of our dynasty, was nearly 18 when he died around 1990.

Of course there seems one big empty spot in this story: no children of my own. In the late 1940s, I experienced two miscarriages very early in the pregnancies, and afterward no pregnancies started, apparently because of some failure in my reproductive system. Clint and I tried everything then known to the medical profession; the modern era of medically arranged pregnancies was not yet available. Since neither of us was interested in adoption or experimental efforts, we reluctantly made our peace with the unhappy situation.

In the 1950s, the political world was fairly quiet. Neither of us had any special friends in the Eisenhower Administration and no interest in a connection to high society. We did attend Truman's Inaugural Ball, a relatively simple affair with the new president and his wife sitting in a box in a big armory. Many of us stopped to shake hands.

But then came John F. Kennedy. The enthusiasm his candidacy engendered had filtered all through the Capitol City. I myself had already made several contacts with him and his famous aide, Ted Sorensen, while JFK was a member of the Senate. He was eager to become better known nationally, so writing an article on a political issue for the *Times* Sunday magazine was a natural target for him and Ted. I also became acquainted with many of the press people working for Kennedy, which is, I believe, why I was asked to write an article in the official Inaugural Program about the history and furnishings in the White House. I also received my usual press tickets to watch the inauguration itself, then held on the East

Front of the Capitol, and to one of the inaugural balls, but by this time this scenario was so old hat to me that I didn't use the tickets, and the weather was too snowy and cold, anyway. But I did attend the First Lady's Luncheon for Newswomen, and by lottery I found myself sitting next to Jackie herself!

Jacqueline Kennedy and Nona at the First Lady's Luncheon for Newswomen, East Room of White House, 1961

In the wake of political change, people I knew personally began emerging in important positions. One was Jim Tobin, my friend from the war years, who was appointed to the Council of Economic Advisers, and another was Letitia (Tish) Baldrige, a Vassar acquaintance, who became Mrs. Kennedy's social secretary. By knowing Jim Tobin—and his boss, Walter Keller—personally, I could reach them by phone for clarification about economic developments, which I did once or twice. They were "official sources" that I valued!

From my personal point of view, however, our connection to Tish Baldrige led to our formal invitation to one of those famous state dinners that defined the Kennedy presidency. That dinner party, honoring André Malraux, the French Minister of Culture, was glamorous and outstanding in every way. Among the guests were some of the country's cultural leaders: Isaac Stern, Leonard Bernstein, George Balanchine, Saul Bellow, Mark

Rothko, Tennessee Williams, and Charles A. Lindbergh, in a rare public appearance. At my dinner table in the main dining room, Isaac Stern was to my left and Stuart Udall was across the round table. Clinton was at another table with (I think) Agnes Mongan and Jackie's mother, Mrs. Auchincloss. This great event also fell on my birthday, so my menu card was quickly filled by all my tablemates (and JFK), and it is still in my possession.

This was a black-tie affair, of course. I wore a robin's-egg blue chiffon gown that I bought at Elizabeth Arden, just for the White House. We entered the Mansion from the small back entrance from the wide lawn where helicopters now land and the Easter Egg Roll occurs. Then we went up to the main floor, with its grand staircase and formal décor. Since I had last seen the interior of the White House during the Truman period, when it was a big hole in the ground surrounded by the familiar walls, I was excited to see the restored State Dining Room and Blue Room looking so glamorous for the seated dinner. The details and pictures of this dinner appeared in Tish Baldrige's 1998 book *In the Kennedy Style: Magical Evenings in the Kennedy White House.*

I was lucky enough to sit at a table directly behind the president, which enabled me a bit later to commit a minor theft. The finale was Kennedy's toast to Malraux, which he ad-libbed to great applause. As the guests rose from their tables and moved toward the Great Hall, I passed just behind Jack Kennedy's seat, and lying there was his dinner program. Well, I just slipped that formal document into my purse and continued out with the crowd. Then the president recognized me and gestured to me to stop with him for a photograph. The menu card, to my surprise, had the unusual (if almost unreadable) personal touch of his scribbles, and much later I discovered that JFK's notes for any speech were extremely rare. That menu now belongs to the JFK Library at Harvard; my pilfered memento was well worth saving! The evening ended with gorgeous music by a very special trio: Isaac Stern, Leonard Rose, and Eugene Istomin. Driving home afterward, Clint and I felt as though we had been dreaming.

President John F. Kennedy, Nona, and Congressman Adam Clayton Powell
in Great Hall of White House, dinner in honor of André Malraux, 1962.
Handwritten note from presidential staff aide to Allen T. Baldwin

In many ways, that glamorous, exciting dinner party marked a turning point for me and Clint—and for the world around us. The 1960s were tumultuous and shocking, reflecting the mood in the country after John Kennedy's election: here was the promise of a new generation and young enthusiasm. Only a year and a half after the Malraux dinner President Kennedy's was assassinated, followed by the murders of Martin Luther King, Jr., and Bobby Kennedy in 1968. This violence was a terrible new threat to us all, I thought; the ugly Vietnam War was costing more and more lives, and more and more dramatic protests were staged against continuing our involvement in it.

In 1963, Clinton and I moved into a new home at 3801 Kanawha Street. With five bedrooms, four baths, a 30-foot living room, large dining room, kitchen, and solarium, this older house was not only larger but a little grander than the semi-detached house on Morrison Street. We had been searching for a home in our Chevy Chase area to accommodate my father, who was learning to navigate life after the amputation of his left leg. Although he had mastered a removable prosthetic leg at age seventy-six, he really couldn't take care of himself when a fever put him in bed for several days. Betty, Tom, and I conferred, and Dad spoke up, too; his final decision was to move to Washington. Clinton was most welcoming, which was the crucial element in the agreement.

So, in 1964, Allen T. Baldwin moved into our guest room and made himself at home as best he could. He never really adjusted to living in our house, where he was not the dominant voice in plans or conversation. We all generally got along well and Dad did enjoy our neighbors as well as walking up to Connecticut Avenue for his new supply of forbidden chocolate candy. For about a year, he happily occupied himself by writing a manual describing a new chemical flux for treating steel in the manufacturing process. One customer bought the manual; the other 499 copies were stored in my attic. I realize now that I could have done more to help him occupy his time after finishing the manual. He worked daily crossword puzzles and played solitaire for hours, so after four years with us, he got bored and asked to move to a newly-opened Quaker retirement home in Sandy Spring, Maryland. He loved his new privacy and unsupervised diet there, but his health was slowly weakening. I was still responsible for supplying his personal needs and transporting him to medical appointments. In 1970, he was hospitalized briefly, and then two days later he keeled over from a heart attack while eating breakfast he had prepared for himself.

My father was a bright man who never achieved as much as he should have (or that I thought he should have), but he never stinted in providing Mother with the best of care. He even bought her that handsome black sealskin coat because, in his view and hers, it was the most elegant garment in the world. The coat was totally impractical, too heavy for her to wear very often. (Eventually the coat became mine. It was almost too heavy for me, too.)

Of course, we were busy getting our lovely new home in good working order. Clint finally had a room he could use for both violin practice and his eternal pile of paperwork on taxes or estate or business matters. I took up needlepoint embroidery, continued dressmaking, and worked full time at the *Times*.

Living in Washington at that moment in history meant living in the middle of violence, ugly political misbehavior, assassinations, anti– and pro–Vietnam War feelings, the social revolution embodied by Woodstock and "free love," and the clashes and triumphs of the civil rights movement. I had to keep up with everything, since the Sunday Review of the Week stayed on the pulse of the daily news everywhere. For instance, I attended President Kennedy's newly enlarged and televised press conferences. I also dictated to a colleague in New York the story of the total traffic gridlock on the city streets as smoke rose over the riot area following the assassination of Martin Luther King, Jr.

That day, all government offices closed by about noon and commuting home was a nightmare. Clinton finally hitched a ride in a car with a colleague and they managed to pick me up by about 3 p.m. Our normal twenty-minute trip took two hours. Our maid, Blanche, was there, frantic with worry about her teenage son, since she lived in the area where serious rioting and looting were underway. We pleaded with Blanche to spend the night with us after we had reached her son by phone and heard he was okay. She went into the pitch-black and empty streets, anyway, and got a ride from a passing car on Military Road. About a half hour later she called to let us know she was home and okay. A few days later a friend brought her back to get milk, meat, eggs, and other groceries for family and friends, since all the stores near her home were still empty.

Almost a week passed before the city of Washington seemed to us to return to normal. But that explosion sharply exposed the depth of black citizens' civil rights problems. Thank goodness we have made so much improvement.

Life at the *Times* was also changing. In 1962, my colleague Cabell Phillips had a sharp argument with Lester Markel—who rarely tolerated dispute—which resulted in Cabell's sudden dismissal. He was immediately re-employed by the main daily operations, and I was left to man the special Sunday desk. Essentially I became the Washington Sunday editor, but I never acquired that title or its appropriate compensation, largely because the whole notion of separate staffing for the Magazine, Review, and other special sections was being abandoned. When that special Sunday staff job ceased to exist in 1974, I didn't look any further. Again, I was never a highly competitive person, and I wasn't wildly ambitious to become a great foreign correspondent or a candidate for punditry about national politics. Personally I was pleased to work for those three decades as a backup reporter, with a finger on many different parts of the Washington scene. I never took a public position in the rising cry for the more equal treatment for women, which, at the *Times*, climaxed in a lawsuit a few years after I retired. I agreed absolutely with the objectives of equal rights and equal pay, but I just didn't have the energy, after thirty-four years at the *Times*, to crank up my irritations into full anger. I feel I did my bit for the "cause" by starting my career in 1940 and successfully proving to many skeptics that a female reporter could work as hard as a male and write professional copy while maintaining personal reserve. In other words, I demonstrated that a professional journalist didn't have to be a man.

Our private lives proceeded as usual. While Dad was living with us, he typically visited Tom or Betty in the summer, and we would take a vacation that included Clinton's mother and aunt Ilona. One year we drove to St. John, New Brunswick, to visit some cousins of the Clinton-Brown clan, which was most enjoyable—the cousins were both hospitable and delightful and the tides of the Bay of Fundy performed with thunderous accuracy. The only tense moment occurred when we reentered the United States at the tiny coastal village of Calais, Maine, reached by back roads and ferries. There was one immigration officer with a small shed for an office, and no other traffic. We were asked to prove our citizenship. Clint and I had driver's licenses, but the two old ladies had nothing and both spoke with accents. I did a lot of talking as they showed checkbooks and every membership card they could find. Ilona had the hardest time, since she had come to America in 1939 as a visitor and was naturalized in 1946. Finally, the officer relented, smiled, and waved us on our way. There was still no one else in sight when we proceeded gaily to Northeast Harbor. Years later, standing in long lines at Heathrow or JFK, I often thought back about this efficient reentry system in Calais.

Amidst all the distractions and crises, Clinton came up with a wonderful idea: *Let's go to Budapest and take his mother and aunt with us!* This was 1965: the Berlin Wall was still standing, but finally Americans could conceivably travel to Eastern Europe. Clint found that the four of us could travel very cheaply on a chartered plane. To me, the idea of taking my lovely mother-in-law and her sister to visit their homeland for the first time since 1936 was truly exciting.

With the help of an Austrian-born travel agent, we got air and train travel reservations to Vienna, Budapest, and London, as well as practical guidance on all the shortages we might face. We all gathered our papers and clothes and stuffed our suitcases with items such as men's socks, scarce over-the-counter medicines, bandages, coffee, and even a boy's American Indian costume for our deprived relatives.

Our first stop was Vienna—a big dose of nostalgia for the two ladies. For them, a trip to Vienna was like a Disney World jaunt today. For about five days we waited, learning that our reserved hotel space in Budapest would not be ready on the original date. Finally, with Gunga and Ilona on tenterhooks, we boarded the train. When we reached Budapest, the reunion of the four siblings was so excited, emotional, and full of rapid-fire conversation that a half hour passed before we managed to get into the tiny Trabant taxis that carried us to the Grand Hotel Margitsziget on an island in the Danube.

Uncle Jeno, Clint's uncle, speaking German, immediately acted as our tour director and soon urged us to go down to the hotel lounge for something to eat. As we walked from the mezzanine down to the main lounge of this formerly grand hotel, we were greeted by a loud blast of "Hello, Dolly!" by the tea dance orchestra. The band must have been warned that some Americans were coming, and they were very enthusiastic about us. We were the only Americans in the hotel during our six-day stay.

Budapest was still a stricken city; it was very dirty and shabby, with many buildings marked with bullet holes, limited electricity, almost no private cars, and no outdoor advertising. We were given ration tickets for meals to be used at only about a half-dozen restaurants. The residents were generally very friendly, perhaps pleased to hear English-speaking people, although few spoke English to us, since German was the second language of Hungary. The amiable, foreign atmosphere was really exciting to me, and my few words of college German came into frequent use.

Clinton and I checked in with the American Embassy the next day and I asked for some help for a travel article about Budapest. I then met Dr. Entz Géza, architectural historian and guardian of many of Budapest's old buildings, which led to a friendship with him and his family that lasted for many years, both in Hungary and Washington. I was exceptionally lucky to have him as my guide throughout the ruins of the Royal Palace on the Várhegy. Abused by Russian and German troops during World War II, it is now fully restored with several museums accommodated within the centuries-old walls.

My memories of this first trip to Hungary are dim or confused with events of later trips, but the general poverty and poor living standards were stunning. The family apartment housed not only Jeno and his wife, Kato, but also his son Sandor and his wife, Itsa, and their son, Gyory. Itsa's kitchen was simply a separate stove, icebox, and washbasin set in the original entrance to the apartment; Kato had use of the main kitchen. Torn-up newspaper constituted the toilet paper in the only bathroom, and the original drawing room served as home to the younger couple day and night, with their son sleeping on a cot in a side room. They had a telephone, I believe, but no radio. Both Itsa and Sandor worked, but Sanyi's health, damaged by pleurisy from being hidden in a basement when the Russian troops came in, was always weak.

The long-held family gravesite had been destroyed and replaced, I believe, by a modern, Soviet-style memorial center where large, individual headstones marked only the graves of Soviet heroes. Although joyous for the siblings to be together again, the whole visit was sad. Mother Brown and Ilona were both aghast at the scruffy, damaged city they loved so much and the family living conditions, yet glad to see everyone still alive. Clinton and I left determined to bring them more help in the future.

Clinton and I intended a return trip a couple of years later, but the very next year the Dutch airline KLM, which was inaugurating a new direct flight from Amsterdam to Budapest and wanted to spread the word, offered me a free trip. During my earlier visit I had written two articles about Hungary for the *Times*'s travel section, and the KLM people had taken note. To avoid flouting ethics standards, I traveled during my vacation time, accepted no stipend from KLM, and made clear that I would not write anything about the trip. I didn't much like the idea of a European jaunt without Clint, but the chance to take additional medications and clothes to the family was irresistible. Of the five or six people in the KLM group, I recall only one couple (a novelist and an opera critic), mostly because we three spent one entire evening enjoying red wine in a tiny wine bar by the Herengracht. Although I spent most of my time in Budapest with Clint's family, I recall that KLM took us on an excursion into the Hungarian plains to a big horse farm where some visiting Bulgars, a troop of horsemen from somewhere in the Carpathians, milked the mares for a special ceremony. This was definitely an unusual sight.

During the following year, 1969, Clint and I planned our own return visit, which launched twenty years of biannual trips to Budapest. We would rent a car in either Frankfurt or Vienna. The trip was sometimes exasperating as we moved into Eastern Europe, waiting in slow lines and enduring full auto inspection to cross the border near Eisenstadt, Austria. In time, we found several favorite inns along the way and practiced our limited German with ever-greater confidence, especially after I took some adult-education language classes. Each year we delivered specially requested items to the family, and we noted small improvements in both hotel accommodations and general living conditions in the city. In our rental car we could take relatives to Lake Balaton, where they owned a tiny, primitive shanty on the water's edge. We also drove Sanyi and Jeno Duma northeast to Eger, a famous Hungarian wine area, which Sanyi had never visited. This put us in the Carpathian Mountains, close to Russia.

My memory of the following events is clear, but the dates are hazy. Clint's uncle, Jeno Duma, died about 1970, and his aunt Anna a couple of years later. Next Kato, Jeno's widow, fell and broke a hip. When we arrived we found her home from the hospital but unable to walk by herself. Apparently no one in Budapest had heard of physical therapy or that new orthopedic aid, the walker, so we brought her one from Washington and she timidly started using it. She told us later that her doctor had neither seen nor heard of such a useful device and that she should rent it out for a good price when she was finished with it.

In 1971, Clinton had the challenging idea of taking his twin nephews, David and Clinton, with us on our next trip. They were sixteen years old, full of curiosity and adventure, and just ready for a broader view of the world. Well, it worked. We had a great time and no real problems, except when those two long-legged teenagers began arm wrestling in the back seat of our rented Renault while we were driving the corkscrew roads through the Austrian Alps. Or the time in Evesham, England, when we stopped to poke around a lovely old church, as Clint and I liked to do. Clint was quietly changing film while sitting in a pew when the twins burst into the nave, chasing each other up and down the pews. Clinton didn't say a word when the church Verger appeared and commanded the boys to behave. The two received a very thorough dressing-down and finally apologized to the Verger, adding that they had both been altar boys at home. They were chagrined, and then much quieter for quite a while.

In 1973, I began to wonder whether we should try to go to a Romanian village called Carensebes, the home of some elderly relatives who were Mother Brown's and Ilona's childhood playmates. The only word about them since before World War II was that the family, who owned the village pharmacy and were leading citizens, had been ousted from their homes by the Communist government. No one knew how or where they were living. My reporter's instincts said, "Let's go find them." We spent a total of four hours crossing the border: two hours to exit Hungary and then two to enter Romania. The main highway was a two-lane paved road shared with farm wagons, goats, and geese. The next day, when we drew into Carensebes—a dusty, bedraggled place with several squares of dull housing and no real business center—we finally located a pharmacy. Since Uncle Edgar, the family patriarch, had been the pharmacist for the area, Clinton went in to seek help. His German did the trick: we found our way fairly quickly to the residence (two rooms of a shabby farmhouse owned by the Sattinger family) and rang the front gate bell.

An old man approached the gate, squinting and apprehensive. Clinton spoke up: "Onkel Edgar, ich bin der sohn von Erszie." We seemed to be apparitions from the past. Onkle Edgar cried, his wife (Tante Klari) cried, Clint and I cried, and soon all the other relatives gathered to peer at us like strangers from another world. I felt intense excitement as I witnessed a family reunited after so many years of war and depravation. With Edgar in charge, we were assigned sleeping quarters with the cousins and Tante Klari fixed some stuffed peppers for our supper. A bottle of schnapps appeared and a merry party filled the evening. No one spoke English.

Thus did my life come to include a whole new family with names such as Müller, Sattinger, and Demeter, and their children and grandchildren. One day, as I sat in their living-bedroom chamber and chatted with Onkel Edgar and Tante Klari, Edgar began searching a huge old desk that had been saved from their original manor house. He finally found a small package carefully wrapped in tissue, examined an object inside, and then handed the parcel to me. There lay an old silver cartouche with the initials *NB* intricately displayed in the center. This had belonged on the household key ring of the long-deceased matriarch of the Müller family, a fearsome but kindly lady named Nina Brancovich. I recognized the name because I knew she had given my mother-in-law a pair of gorgeous diamond earrings as a wedding present in 1911. With this hugely sentimental gift, I was truly admitted to this unusual, warm-hearted, and long-suffering family. The NB cartouche hangs now from a silver chain around my neck, and is a truly favorite piece of jewelry. (I also wear daily one of those big diamonds on a ring I had made after Mother Brown died. She had the stones from those earrings set into separate rings, and the other went to Polly, her other daughter-in-law. Later I had a new ring made to hold both the Duma diamond and my smaller diamond from Clinton.)

When we returned from that year's trip, we found Mother Brown to be very ill and requiring constant attention. We knew she had been failing slowly, but her doctor told us not to worry when we left for Europe. Poor advice! We moved her fast, first from her crowded apartment to our house. Clint then had a forceful phone conversation with the doctor, who quickly ordered a special blood test, which showed that she had well-advanced acute myelogenous leukemia. On the following day, she was moved to Sibley Hospital. Two months later, she died at eighty-five years of age.

When we all finished the ceremonial aspect of mourning, we had to make quick arrangements for Ilona, who could not afford to keep their apartment. Happily Ilona came to live with us. She was an easy guest, quiet and undemanding, although she still smoked cigarettes. At first she was depressed by her sister's death, but she was also excited by our report from Carensebes about her childhood chums. So we ended up planning another trip with her and Nona (Nikki) Brown, age sixteen, the youngest of Jim and Polly's six children, who was rebellious and having difficulties at her private school. Family discord made her situation very troubled. After I had a chat with the school's headmistress, I proposed taking Nikki with us to Europe to give her breathing space and maybe a better sense of direction. Thus in 1974, the four of us took off for Europe, with no advance notice to the family that Ilona would be with us. You can imagine the surprise and exuberant enthusiasm when we arrived, as well as the excited frustration of young Nikki, who was swamped by all the Hungarian and German chatter. I remember especially a dinner party given by cousins Elemer and Klari Demeter in their small Budapest apartment. There were eight or nine of us and four languages: a rough stew for an American teenager; Nikki still talks about her utter bewilderment at that meal. However, when we arrived in Carensebes a few days later, nineteen-year-old Marianna Hortolani, the English-speaking granddaughter of Edgar and Klari, was there, resolving Nikki's communication crisis.

Our stay in Carensebes coincided with the huge Watergate political crisis in Washington. One evening, Edgar managed to tune into the BBC on his very ancient—and illegal—radio to hear the sudden announcement that President Nixon had resigned. Nikki whooped with joy, Clinton and I were very pleased, but Onkel Edgar was puzzled and saddened, since he liked Nixon's way of dealing with Russia and understood nothing about our domestic politics. It was surreal to me to hear this incredible news as I sat in a shabby farmhouse in a Romanian village, an alienated communist neighborhood totally devoid of contact with the rest of the world.

Meanwhile, Marianna and Nikki became immediate buddies. Marianna had just been married and her husband, a German of Romanian origin, had returned to Marburg, Germany, where he was a university student. Within the next decade, almost all of the Romanian relatives followed her to West Germany, legally or illegally. Two grandsons in the Sattinger family actually sneaked across the Danube by rowboat and then swam and crawled through marshes to reach Belgrade, Yugoslavia. They found the German Embassy, where, to prove their identities, they offered the case number of their father's conviction of high economic crimes against the Romanian government. (Amnesty International had helped to win his release.) Apparently, German diplomacy kept careful records and thus verified Reinhard's and Walter's identifications. By the next day, they were in Munich, from where they finally called their parents in Carensebes by phone: they all qualified as "Volksdeutsch" under German law and were welcomed "home."

The rest of this immigrant family left Romania by overstaying visitor visas or waiting years for official exit permits from Romania. Marianna was legally allowed to join her husband, and the next year we visited them in their university students' apartment. Today, I keep in touch with and have visited Marianna and her husband and two children several times, as well as Clarike and Bubi Sattinger and their sons, Reini and Waltie.

Becoming part of this extended European family has been a great joy for me. I also am happy that Clinton and I helped reestablish communication between not only the Carensebes group and Budapest, but also with the Polish cousins in Warsaw, Poland.

Clint had a great uncle who married a Polish woman and settled there in the nineteenth century. Jeno had received only one letter from his Polish cousin since World War II and had just one street address. In 1978, we joined a National Press Club travel group for a trip to Warsaw, Budapest, and Prague, which we couldn't resist. As soon as we had checked into our Warsaw hotel, we set out, map in hand, to find the address. It was actually only a few blocks away, with the Wiszniewska apartment clearly lettered. Our knock on the door elicited a loud warning bark, and then a timid female voice. The door opened and Clint, once again, quickly identified himself as the son of Erszie Duma. The woman was Ada Wiszniewska, granddaughter of Clint's great-uncle. Ada almost exploded with excitement and phoned immediately to her son, a linguist with fluent English. Witek materialized in a few minutes, and out of drawers poured stacks of old family photographs, most of which were already familiar to Clint. I guess life in Warsaw was as dreary and impoverished as life in Carensebes; the exuberant reaction at our sudden appearance was so similar. We had a good visit on this first trip and made another trip about ten years later. Witek was always a generous, cheerful host; we met his wife, a theater manager, and children; and Ada and her sister Wanda exchanged Christmas cards with us. Additionally, Witek and I send long yearly reports to each other. I keep hoping to find a way for my Brown nieces and nephews to embrace these new family relationships.

By 1980, we had made ten trips to Hungary and decided the time had come to take a closer look at England and the Continent. A gift of the handsome, illustrated book *Great Houses of Britain* by Nigel Nicolson became our travel guide, as it emphasized the historic importance of major buildings from Lands End to John O'Grote's (by way of Cambridge, Norfolk, York and Durham, the Lake Country, Edinburgh, and London). Our first trip to England focused on the Channel ports where Clinton and his Landing Craft group had been stationed for the D-Day invasion. During the next dozen years, we must have made at least six or seven trips to England, Ireland, Scotland, and Wales, plus two extended trips: one to France and one to Italy with my good friends Mary Munroe and Enid Hyde as tour directors. Since I never kept a diary, and I no longer have my Michelin guides, I am not sure what we saw and when we saw it, but I do know we had a great time, especially when we were driving ourselves and stopping often in small inns, without reservations. In Wales, we actually got a room in the gatehouse to the Cathedral Close. In Bristol, we were assigned the Anne Boleyn room of Bristol Castle; in York, we stayed in the "Judge's Chambers"; and in Ireland, we had a tiny upstairs rooms in a boarding house, which afforded a front seat to the evening concert on the town square as the sun set at 10:30 p.m. In those years after retirement I did only a modest amount of writing for the *Times*. I especially enjoyed reporting the medieval Passion Play performed at York Minster every four years. Like the more famous one at Oberammergau, this play involved a cast of villagers and professional actors, farm animals, and medieval church chants and rituals, and occupied ancient central York for its stage. I could have pursued many other possibilities for stories—the turmoil surrounding Ronald Reagan's visit to Tipperary, or the Scottish defense guns installed on the North Sea to ward off any German attacks, or

Stonehenge before it was walled in—but I much preferred just traveling and learning for pleasure. Freelance work was too time consuming.

We also made many friends as we traveled and visited with them later. Beryl and Leonard Archer and Dr. George and Zeida Jarrett, whom we met at a country inn in Dorset, were so congenial that we not only visited them later on that same trip, but returned to entertain them at our favorite English country house, Hambleton Hall in Lincolnshire. In Scotland, a young couple, Ian and Isabel Thompson, whom we'd met at a wedding in Washington, hospitably took us under their wing several times. We always managed to see the Harmans, too, who lived in a charming Queen Anne cottage—which they had improved themselves—near Basingstoke. And Dr. Pamela Davies, a cousin of Clinton's who lived in London, became truly a very good friend. Sad to say, both Kakki Harman and Pamela Davies have died recently.

In addition to travel, there was much "ordinary" daily activity: repainting our house and improving our garden; quick trips to places like the Smokies in North Carolina and Mount Washington; big Brown-Langdon family reunions in Chicago; Sheridan, Wyoming; and Rhinebeck, New York. Also, I became much too involved personally with a neighbor who was showing early Alzheimer's symptoms and couldn't cope with her legal or medical needs. This gave me a vivid exposure to one of our nation's mounting social problems today. We were both so busy, I wondered how we ever had time to work!

CHAPTER 5

The Beginning of the End

In the late 1970s, I found myself strangely exhausted. I'm not normally introspective, but suddenly I realized I needed help. Since 1970, my father and Clint's mother had died, Ilona had died after three years of living with us, and my own life had altered sharply after the rather abrupt end to my thirty-four-year career with the *Times*. That is when Dr. Wesley Oler took charge of my health. In short order he stabilized me and new interests rose to the surface.

Meanwhile, Clinton yearned to escape the bureaucratic jungle, so he retired from the Justice Department. By 1980, we were in a position to do what we wanted and could afford. We joined friends in the Friday Evening Dance Group, which held three formal ballroom dances (we both loved dancing) each year; we took an art history course at the National Gallery; I became increasingly interested in Colonial Williamsburg and its annual antiques forum; and we frequently joined with neighbors for drinks before dinner. In fact, many neighbors became close friends: the Splains, Morandas, McCartneys, Abbotts, McManuses, and Van Dusens, along with their children and, now, grandchildren. I am not sure what happened precisely in each year of this period both at home and abroad, but I do remember that 1980 was particularly crazy: we went to Greece with the Women's National Press Club, sightseeing around Athens and then cooling off with a week of cruising through the famous Greek Islands before visiting Istanbul and heading back to Athens. Then we flew directly north to Budapest for our biannual family visit. The climax for the year—or so we thought—was our amazing ten-day trip to India, sponsored by the National Press Club. With a per-person price of $1500 that covered air travel overseas and within India, all hotel expenses, and meals, this was a chance we couldn't refuse! It was crazy—too much, too fast—but we went.

We arrived in New Delhi at dawn and were greeted at our hotel with a swirl of musicians and elephants in ceremonial dress. From that moment until we boarded our return flight ten days later, there wasn't a moment without something for us to do. From New Delhi we flew to Jaipur, Udaipur, Aurangabad, and then Bombay. Each hotel trotted out its finest culinary offerings to impress the 60 press people in our group, and we were shown the key historic sights of India: the Taj Mahal, the Pink City, the Palace of the Winds, the ancient caves near Aurangabad, and even a burning ghat in Bombay. We also could see and smell the overwhelming poverty in the cities, such as the many clusters of families squatting and eating in the area around the Great Gate in Bombay. By the end we were all exhausted and couldn't eat another bite of Indian food, despite its high quality. The trip was memorable for me simply for the intense glimpse of a very important country that I'll probably never have another chance to visit.

Then, a few months later, I was diagnosed with breast cancer. That was obviously shattering news. I found the lump in one breast myself but said nothing because Clint and I were leaving the next day to drive to Rochester to spend Thanksgiving with Betty and her family. I saw no need to spoil the holiday for everyone, so I simply made an appointment to see Dr. Oler right after we got home. I told Clinton the night we returned to Washington. My suspicion was quickly corroborated by X-ray and needle biopsy. Surgery was scheduled for a few days later. In those days, lumpectomies were novel and seemed very risky so I proceeded with the standard modified radical mastectomy. The surgeon, Dr. Neville Connolly, greeted me with a hello from his wife, a college friend of mine, so the event felt rather relaxed to me. After the surgery, I received a course of chemotherapy for safety's sake, so I spent most of 1981 receiving biweekly chemo-cocktail injections. The chemo didn't really bother me, except for fatigue. However, I brooded some about the future and worried whether I would outlive the estimated five-year survival period, but somehow I never seriously considered a bad ending for myself, an attitude borne of my congenital optimism, I guess. We had long planned as a summer guest the young Gyory Duma, a student about nineteen years old. I enjoyed his visit very much. We drove him down the Skyline Drive and took him to Williamsburg, New York City, and the Atlantic Beach Club. Gyory seemed quite excited about it all, but he clearly missed his girlfriend back home and also was annoyed that we wouldn't let him hitchhike to the Grand Canyon!

I took it easy for the next year, but in 1983 I was ready to sign up for a tour of Brazil, a short, cheap trip entirely by air and including a stop in the new capital, Brasilia. The greatest shock to me was the ultra-modern, air-conditioned hotel in Manaus, an urban flyspeck on the river through trackless Amazon forest. Our first stop was this deluxe hotel, with swimming pools and gourmet meals, surrounded by rain forest. We all took a short walk through some well-cleared jungle to a swimming hole complete with piranha! The capital, Brasilia, struck me as totally uninteresting and unwelcoming, despite its architectural perfection. Nonetheless Brazil looked splendid, and the country had turned into a huge business enterprise. Overall we had fun; the atmosphere was all new to Clinton, and my stamina was perfectly normal.

So we started planning more travels, beginning with a real blockbuster: a nineteen-day trip to France, sponsored by the Sulgrave Club, a Washington ladies' club I had joined in 1983. I had long wanted to see more of France than Paris, and this itinerary included the Loire Valley, Dijon, Lyons, the southeast area near Chinon, and then Avignon and Nice. French historic preservation specialists had arranged visits for us to meet the owners of houses, manor houses, castles, and other ancient dwellings and to learn what the French were doing to preserve the country's aging architectural patrimony. Mary Monroe and Enid Hyde, both friends of mine and experts on the history of the region, truly enriched the whole experience. We ate well, too, at several four-star restaurants, and we stayed at lovely country inns. I felt I had absorbed a year's worth of cultural education. When our tour ended in Nice, Clinton and I added our own side trip to visit a college classmate, Peggy Ferguson, at her Provence country home. We then spent three more days, with her guidance, checking out Roman ruins, small villages, and local food markets. Our hostess was a superb cook who would create our evening meal from the fresh produce we chose earlier in the day. Dinner was informal, out on the terrace overlooking her swimming pool and fields of blooming lavender. What a glorious way to live! A couple of years later, a similarly long group tour took us to Italy, where we concentrated on Palladian architecture.

Nona on camel in Tunisia, circa 1982

In the early '90s, we still balanced a good deal of traveling with our busy schedule at home. Clinton had become interested in local historic preservation issues (mostly to try to save his grandmother's home in historic downtown Washington) and local politics. At one point he even ran for a seat on the D.C. City Council, but he did not win much public support. I found my own time absorbed by my new Sulgrave Club membership, which led to my being asked almost immediately to help with the monthly bulletin. I was able to assist in a number of small ways, drawing on my professional career, and ultimately spent ten years working on the Sulgrave monthly newsletter. This involvement led to two terms of service on the Board of Governors, the controlling body for this handsome and successful ladies' club near Dupont Circle. To me, this was all a huge learning experience, meeting many new women who were bright, active, hard-working ladies of the category denominated (derisively, I feel) today as stay-at-home moms. Many of these new friends—some still good personal friends—worked as hands-on managers of the historic Wadsworth building owned by the club and the amenities expected by the 800 or so members. The Sulgrave Club is where Clinton and I celebrated our fiftieth wedding anniversary and where I celebrated my ninetieth birthday. Clinton was especially fond of our evening lectures by prominent government, diplomatic, or journalism leaders. The Club has been a very important force in my life for thirty years now, supplying intellectual stimulation, superior meals, and lots of fun in a rather intellectual ambience. As I write, of course, my use of the Club is confined to weekly bridge lessons and maybe an occasional lecture-luncheon, with taxis for transportation!

In about 1990, Clinton and I began to notice signs that we were getting old. My stamina faded every time I climbed a flight of stairs; Clinton began having rheumatic problems and endured a terrible siege with temporal arteritis. The only treatment for this dangerous condition was high doses of cortisone for forty days to knock out the arterial infection. These also knocked out his brain. After a frantic and confusing ten days, he finally normalized, and the infection was gone. To reward ourselves for surviving this crisis, we went to England with John and Pat Willis to celebrate her seventieth birthday and show these good friends our favorite spots in Wales and Lancashire. This trip was slow-paced and restful, and happily I was able to do all the driving, since Clint was still quite shaky. I treasure the memory.

Brother Tom Baldwin, sister Betty Baldwin Montbach, Nona, and Clinton at golden wedding anniversary party, Sulgrave Club, Washington, DC, 1994

Our last chapter, really, began at Christmas 1994 with a dramatic opening scare: I fell on the carpeted grand stairway of the Sulgrave Club after an exuberant Christmas dinner. My left shoulder was fractured, so we spent a long night in the emergency room of Georgetown Hospital. Luckily I needed only a heavy sling for my left arm, so we proceeded with our normal Christmas activities, which were mostly at Lexie's house. When I was allowed to drive again months later, I parked at the Saks Fifth Ave parking lot for a physical therapy session when a truly freak accident intervened: the car door slammed closed on my left foot! So now a broken ankle—and full cast—took over my life. I used a wheelchair to move around the house and gave Clinton cooking instructions while I sat in the kitchen doorway. During the winter, I read *No Ordinary Time* by Doris Kearns Goodwin, which introduced me to the lively political history of people and events in my own lifetime. By May I was ready to get going again, namely to Yale for Clinton's fiftieth reunion, which was a time for fun and old friends. In the fall, Enid Hyde phoned to invite us to join a small group for a trip to Helsinki, St. Petersburg, and Moscow. Since the Kremlin was the one place Clinton wanted to see before we gave up foreign travel for good, we signed up. The itinerary started with just a quick look at Helsinki, then five days in the fascinating old imperial Russian capital, and finally Moscow and the Bolshoi Ballet. We got tired. I became weary while climbing so many stairs without railings, and Clinton heedlessly wandered away from the group in the Hermitage, but the trip was essentially all exciting and colorful . . . .

Until the last day. We were descending the steps to the Pushkin Museum. I couldn't see the bottom step—so down I went. I was immediately aware that something was wrong with my left leg; it was clear that I needed medical help. Enid, who knew the Russian Museum staff, enlisted help in locating an American medical center and learned that the relatively new clinic operated by New York–Presbyterian Hospital was not only open on a Sunday afternoon, but would send a vehicle to pick me up. It was a small Polish trabant, and it bumped its way over potholes to the clinic building. The doctor on duty immediately called in his x-ray technician and senior nurse. The X-ray confirmed a fracture of the left hip (actually, the intertrochanteric bone), and we were quickly told that the nearest place for its repair was Helsinki! (At that time, medical advancements in Russia did not include hip repair or replacement.)

That whole evening was a mad scramble, with phone calls to Helsinki to arrange a medical evacuation plane, to a hospital and doctor for my care, to my credit card servers to figure a way to combine my available credit to cover the $17,000 prepaid cost of the medevac service, and to my orthopedic doctor in Washington, who ordered the move to Helsinki as medically necessary. The clinic doctor and Clinton handled all this arranging—in just about six hours. Enid managed all the travel and suitcase business, as well as sandwiches for our supper. At about midnight Clinton and I and our luggage left the Moscow airport with minimum passport formalities or luggage inspection. The plane was small: Clinton and I and a Finnish doctor filled the cabin, with me lying in a litter on the side wall. I was well morphined and slept during the flight, then I woke up in a gleaming white hospital admissions area, welcomed in English by a kindly nurse in traditional white garb. I was immediately whisked to my room, which included an extra bed so Clinton could stay with me. The repair surgery—with the essential part a large screw—was performed the next day under Finland's public health system, and physical therapy started immediately. Less than two weeks after admission we were on our way back to Washington on Finnair, equipped with a pair of elbow crutches and some Tylenol.

I was lucky to become quite adept at walking with an elbow crutch. A few weeks later, my sister, Betty, died suddenly in an automobile accident, and Clinton and I flew to Rochester, where I was able to participate in family mourning plans. Christmas was quiet. Then, in early January, Washington was overwhelmed with a massive blizzard: twenty-five inches of snow with no snow plows on the streets. The whole city shut down. Clint tried to pick up our Sunday newspapers from the deep snow, but nearly collapsed from the effort, ashen and short of breath. He felt shaky all day. When Clint's temperature soared to 103°F the next afternoon, I consulted by phone with his doctor (who was also snowed in), who said the fever meant pneumonia and I must get him to the hospital immediately. "How can I do that?" I asked. "Just call 911," replied the doctor, "and hope they can get to you." So I called 911, as well as several neighbors who pitched in with shovels and cleared our sidewalks all the way around the corner so that we could get out of the house. The emergency vehicle was a fire truck. After nearly skidding into parked cars, the fire truck halted at the corner of 38th and Kanawha, just a short walk for us both. We were hoisted into the rear section of the cab and off we went, with sirens blaring, to Sibley Hospital. There was no other traffic on the road.

Clinton was admitted right away. By about 10 p.m., all was under control, except where I could go. Luckily a volunteer with a four wheel-drive car was at the Sibley emergency entrance, and he took me to the nearby apartment complex where my sister-in-law lived. Two weeks passed before I could safely go home; my car had been entombed for all that time.

Needless to say, that period was anxious. Clinton was very ill and in intensive care for several days. Then his strength began to return, and so at the end of January he was released to come home. When he arrived at the house, however, he seemed suddenly so weak that I wondered what had happened to him overnight. His doctor was mystified, but he supposed that the homecoming event had been tiring. So home was where he was, thank goodness, when, early the next morning, he stopped breathing. I had been with him all night and at the end even tried CPR. Frantic emergency efforts could not help him: he had died of a heart attack. (From an autopsy I learned later that he had a rapidly advancing case of leukemia, which underlay the illness.)

Clinton and I had rarely discussed future plans, but he often said that he didn't want a fancy funeral home scenario and preferred to be buried in a setting more personal than Arlington National Cemetery. So I planned a memorial service for him at All Saints Episcopal Church, where he had worshiped for years, and then we quietly buried his ashes in a Quaker burying ground in West Chester, where my family had a plot. Father Gregory Maletta, a friend and priest from All Saints, presided at the interment. It was restful and peaceful. He was eighty-two years old.

Widowhood meant many changes. My lifetime companion—the person I turned to for warmth and comfort, for answers and decisions, for trust and honesty—was gone. That loss is still there. I had no personal difficulty in taking control of financial matters, since I had written all the checks for household bills for years. I knew about tax returns and had long before established my own personal credit standing and sense of personal strength. Without Clinton, nothing was the same—but our home and my life went on.

Less than a month after the funeral, part of the roof of the house blew off. A big sheet of tin sailed over the side porch and settled within inches of my car! Here was my first crisis. I turned to a nephew who lived very near, but he wasn't home. Then I called neighbors, who were wonderful, moving the huge metal sheet to a grassy spot, and then I called our roofer. Even on Sunday afternoon, he came right away and tarped the open area. Then I was able to relax. I realized that family, friends, neighbors, and tradesmen were my support group of the future.

And so began my new life. I kept up (but reduced) my Sulgrave Club involvement and plunged into arranging home maintenance projects, such as painting the house, fixing the chronic leaks in the basement, and rebuilding and replanting the north edge of our property. All this kept me busy for several years, but my own good health began to slip. A double bout of bronchitis put me in bed for a while and left me with an asthma condition and a lifelong dependency on inhalers.

The McCartney family deserves a special aside in my life story. As a young family, they moved to Kanawha Street at about the time their fourth child, Annie, was born. At age three, Annie discovered our kittens and became such a frequent visitor to our house for the next four years that we described ourselves as her "in loco grand parentis." Many years later, when Jack learned that I was housebound after back surgery, he volunteered to get my grocery list every Friday and then pick up the food when he and his wife did their own weekly marketing. Then Jack would deliver the produce on Saturday mornings, which led to brief chats and then longer visits and long-running discussions about politics such as the Obama campaign and Iraq war, health problems, mutual friends, philosophy, and life in general. Even today our conversations continue when he drops in to see me on Thursday afternoons. I feel truly privileged to know Jack and Marion, an architect and a nurse-midwife, and their four creative children, all of whom are happily busy helping others in so many ways. They certainly have helped me!

I also acquired a major new interest by going with Mary Louise Day to the Chautauqua Institution's summer programs and learning about this amazing resort in western New York. Because her family had been living in nearby Erie, Mary Louise was familiar with Chautauqua's stimulating intellectual thinking as well as its charming atmosphere. I first joined her in the summer of 1997 and continued every year I could until 2006. Chautauqua is a place for walking, but as I got older and had more orthopedic problems, the long trip by plane or car became too arduous for both of us. She and I both still miss our summer dose of outstanding lectures on public issues.

Health problems, unfortunately, had begun to dominate my life. I had always taken my good health for granted, but that changed, beginning with the broken shoulder, ankle, and hip in 1995, all involving replacement surgeries. In 1997, after a good time at Chautauqua, I returned to Washington and discovered I had a serious colon blockage. Luckily, the corrective surgery was performed quickly. The next year, pain in my left shoulder became unbearable because the fracture had not mended normally, so bone was rubbing on bone. The joint had to be replaced, calling again for surgery and a long spell of physical therapy. I finally got back about 75 to 80 percent normal usage of my left arm.

A short trip to England and Scotland in 1999 with friends from the Maryland Historical Society group taught me that clearly I was losing stamina and couldn't handle stairs anymore. By 2000, I was in deep trouble: my damaged hip was failing and the nerves in my lumbar spine were screaming at me. First was a hip replacement and about six months later the laminectomy and fusion of my lumbar vertebrae. This blow was almost a knockout.

As I recovered slowly at home, I began to recognize that I was leaning too heavily on family for help, even after weeks in Sibley Hospital and rehab plus a month in a nursing home. I had to ask Betsy to come live with me until I was strong enough to prepare meals. Betsy agreed immediately, but as the month wore on, the situation became very stressful, especially since she was working full time at a bookstore. This was not a feasible long-term solution for my needs. I quickly realized that I should place myself somewhere with health care at hand.

As I thought this through, I knew my brother was in no position to try to take me in. Anyhow, I wanted to continue my personal way of life as long as possible. I also knew I didn't want to move twice, first to an apartment and then, inevitably, to a nursing home. Reluctantly, yet firmly, I decided to sell my lovely house and move to Grand Oaks, a new facility on the grounds of Sibley Hospital with assisted living apartments. All my doctors—and my friends and familiar social life—would be nearby. In October 2003, I sold the house and made the big move from large house to two-room apartment, bringing with me all my favorite furniture.

I have been here for eight years now; time has flown by and I have never regretted the move. When Mary Louise decided to sell her house and move to Grand Oaks at the same time I did, we each made a beneficial decision to put ourselves in reach of immediate health care while living our own lives within the constantly changing limits imposed by a growing assortment of pills. We are lucky to have such a solid friendship.

Accessible health care was really what I needed. Within one year, a pacemaker was installed to calm my heart fibrillation. Then pain returned, this time in my right hip and lower back, and the surgeons took over again.

First came the hip replacement (this required two major operations within four weeks because the femur cracked while I was still in the hospital, so the whole procedure had to be repeated after repairing the femur) and next came the corrective lumbar spine fusion. This time I recovered in my own comfortable apartment with nursing and meal service provided. This was truly a stress-free and comfortable six-month recovery. I was lucky to have moved here when I did.

This place has a life of its own, accommodating many interesting fellow residents over the years, with some inevitably dropping by the wayside. I get out as much as I would like, such as to Shakespeare theater, symphony concerts, or dinner at nearby restaurants. Since I stopped driving three years ago, good friends and acquaintances fill the gap. We have one private driver, a retired man who likes to help older people with errands and social events. He actually drove Mary Louise and me up to Vassar for our seventieth reunion in June 2009. She and I also maintained our original Saturday night widow's dinner date, which began before 2003. The inclusion of two newcomers, who are still driving, made it very lively. Recently the weekly party went into abeyance only because the principal driver was hospitalized. I play bridge as often as possible, and we enjoy good company at the lunch and dinner tables; this is not a stodgy place! We keep up with the news and read a lot of books. My nieces Betsy and Lexie come often just to visit or to bring me toiletries; they are my family mainstay, on the spot. Other Brown and all Baldwin relations check in frequently, in person or by phone. And in 2008 I lured my entire family—thirty-four relatives and spouses—to a glorious, glamorous dinner party at the Sulgrave Club. This was an exciting evening for all of us. But, truth be told, my social calendar has more medical appointments than anything else, and my interest in going out has diminished. Now my health is quite stable, and my key doctors (internal, heart, and pulmonary) are very good at preventative and palliative medicine.

For me, the last third of the twentieth century was placid, like a deep lake guarded by a natural calm. An underground spring, called the new technology, kept gaining strength and broke the surface, changing everything! A life dominated by digital screens with those little jumpy numbers, with all society held together by wires and websites, and wealth measured by billions of icons is not for me. It is not only incomprehensible but unreal! So I ended the twentieth century in a protective crouch, choosing not use a computer. That was probably stupid. I do marvel at the amazing things the new industries are doing. I am still compelled to know what is happening in the world, read two newspapers daily, and watch PBS news in the evening. Friends, both old and new, stop by or phone me frequently—such Mary Louise Day, Jack McCartney, Nancy Martin, or Ursula McManus. I may be bored, but never lonely, and a good book is always at hand.

How long this benign life will last is the unanswerable question. I was excited that all members of the Baldwin family (husbands, wives, and children) assembled here for my ninetieth birthday party, but I am not planning to issue save-the-date invitations for 2013. I am lucky to have had journalism, economics, and political science as my windows on the fleeting decades of the twentieth century—and now I cannot decide whether to cheer or moan for the future. Surely human beings can find a way to live together peaceably and enjoy the miracles of our planet. I am, at the end, a hopeful humanist.

January 2012